© 2025 Hidayah Kids
All rights reserved.

No part of this publication may be reproduced, stored, or shared in any form without written permission from the publisher — except brief excerpts for educational or review purposes.

Author & illustrator: Hidayah Asfand
Publisher: Hidayah Kids

Hardcover - ISBN: 978-1-969312-09-0
Paperback - ISBN: 978-1-969312-15-1
EBook - ISBN: 978-1-969312-10-6

Website: www.hidayahkids.com
Email: info@hidayahkids.com
First Edition – 2025

About the Super Muslim Heroes Series

The Super Muslim Heroes Series features inspiring true stories from early Islam, crafted for Muslim children.

It highlights the bravery and faith of the companions of Prophet Muhammad ﷺ, showcasing their courage and sacrifice in engaging, age-appropriate narratives. Based on authentic Islamic sources (Tafsir Hadith and Sirah books), the series includes footnotes for further exploration.

Aimed at readers aged 7–15, it encourages young readers to understand heroism through Iman, character, and courage, making it enjoyable for the entire family.

❤️✨ Dedication

To my beloved Baba,
Who was blessed with a vision for this book while seated in Riyad al-Jannah (inside the Prophet's Mosque – Madina Munawwara),
and lovingly guided me every step of the way.

To my loving Mama,
Whose quiet strength, design ideas and endless du'as made every page possible.

And to my little sisters, Emaan and Zarsha,
For being my biggest cheerleaders — and my favorite listeners.

— *Hidayah Asfand*

Is This Just a Story?

Not at all!

Unlike most story books, every name, every du'ā, every moment in this book is real — taken from authentic Islamic sources like Tafsir Ibn Kathir, Sahih Bukhari, Sahih Muslim, and Sirah Ibn Hisham.

The Battle of Badr happened on 17th Ramadan, 2 AH (13 March 624 CE) — over 1,400 years ago.

Only 313 Muslims stood against 1,000 enemy soldiers.

It was a war that changed the history — not through power, but through faith.
These were the real superheroes.
And their light still guides us today.

Contents

Chapter 1: The Trouble in Makkah — 13

Chapter 2: The Call to Badr — 25

Chapter 3: The Small Army of Believers — 41

Chapter 4: The Young Muslim Superheroes — 53

Chapter 5: Victory from Allah — 95

✷ Meet the Brave Story Tellers ✷

Before we start the journey back in time to 7th century Mecca...
Let's meet the four friends who will take us there!

Hidayah

The wise big sister. Hidayah is calm, thoughtful, and always ready with a story — with authentic references! She loves reading books and finds joy in learning about the Prophet ﷺ and his Companions, whom she sees as her greatest role models.

When the stars are out and the lanterns are glowing, she opens her scroll and softly says,

"This isn't just a story... it really happened."

Shujāʿ - the Baby Camel

The brave (and slightly confused) one.
Shujāʿ is full of imagination — sometimes too much! He claims he once flew to Madinah... on a flying scroll. "Do camels need passports for time travel?".... He cracks jokes, makes everyone laugh, and just when you think he's being silly... he'll say something surprisingly deep.

Emaan

The curious one — full of energy, questions, and big expressions.

Emaan loves to act out the stories with flair and fun.

Her playful spirit brings joy — and sometimes even corrects the camel's wild ideas!

Zarsha

The baby of the team. Zarsha doesn't say much, but when she does... it's adorable.

She shouts "Bisma-bis!" when she means "Bismillah," and claps when the story gets exciting. Her tiny voice, sparkling eyes, and endless copying of her sisters make every moment cuter.

These four friends are about to travel back over 1,400 years...

With a glowing scroll, hearts full of curiosity and ready to learn — their journey through faith, bravery, and the early days of Islam is about to begin.

🚀 A Special Book Begins...

The room was warm and quiet. A soft rug covered the floor, and tiny stars twinkled through the window. Cushions lay in a circle, and in the middle sat Hidayah, holding something wrapped in a shiny indigo ribbon — a long scroll with golden edges.

She looked calm, focused — like a young teacher ready to begin.

Hidayah (gently untying the ribbon, voice soft but excited):
"This scroll is special, you know. It has something more powerful than stories... it holds the truth. Every name, every du'a, every tear — it all really happened."

Shujā' the Baby Camel (raising an eyebrow and whispering dramatically):
"Wait... are there real lions in there? Like, rawr lions? Or just lion-hearted people?"

Emaan (grinning and pointing):
"If there are lions, I'm hiding behind your hump, Shujā'!"

Shujāʿ (pretending to puff up with pride):
"Excuse me! I'm a scholar-camel. I teach bravery, not block it with my behind!"
Everyone burst into laughter. Even little Zarsha clapped with delight.

Hidayah (unrolling the scroll, eyes glowing):
"Okay team... are you ready for a journey through time?".
She paused and looked at each of them.
"...To a time when the city of Makkah was filled with idols, not Iman (faith).
A time when few believed, but the believers were stronger than mountains."
She lowered the scroll gently to the floor, the golden letters shimmering in the lantern light.

Zarsha (clapping): "We go flyyyyyy!"

Hidayah (raising her hand like a tour guide):

"We're not flying in planes — we're time-traveling with our imaginations and our hearts. Come on, let's go back in time — to the city where the light of Islam first began to shine…"

📍 Year: 610 CE / Year 13 Before Hijrah
📍 Place: Makkah

Our mission begins… now.

And with giggles, grins, and glowing hearts… the journey began.

CHAPTER 1
THE TROUBLE IN MAKKAH

'Say la ilaha illallah and you will succeed'

Ahad! Ahad!

A long time ago, in the heart of a vast desert, there stood a city called Makkah — surrounded by tall brown mountains and hot sandy lands. In the centre of this city stood something very special: the Kaaba, the House of Allah.

The Kaaba wasn't just a building. It was a place of worship built long ago by two noble prophets — Prophet Ibrahim (A.S.) and his son Prophet Ismail (A.S.). Together, they raised its walls with their own hands, saying:

> "Our Lord! Accept [this] from us..."
> — Surah Al-Baqarah, 2:127

It was built to worship Allah alone, the One True God. But over time, something very sad had happened. The people of Makkah had forgotten about Allah. Instead of worshiping Him, they placed idols—statues made of stone, wood, or clay—all around the Kaaba. They gave these idols names. They asked them for help. But idols cannot hear. They cannot speak. They cannot help anyone.

Only Allah, the One who created the skies, the stars, and everything in between — is worthy of worship.

🕋 The Prophet Muhammad ﷺ Begins His Mission

Then came the moment that changed everything.

At the age of 40, Prophet Muhammad ﷺ, known throughout Makkah for being truthful and kind, received a powerful message from Allah through Angel Jibreel (A.S.).

The message was simple and clear:

"THERE IS NO GOD BUT ALLAH"

The Prophet ﷺ quietly began sharing the message with his family...

Then with his close friends...

Then with the people of Makkah.

"SAY LA ILAHA ILLALLAH AND YOU WILL SUCCEED."
— SAHIH MUSLIM

But the leaders of Makkah were not happy.

They were worried.

"What if people stop buying idol statues?"

"What if we lose our power?"

So instead of listening to the truth, they became angry.

What did they do?

The people who believed in the Prophet ﷺ were called Muslims. But the idol-worshippers started hurting them.

Here are some sad things that happened:
- They called the Prophet ﷺ a liar and a magician.
- They threw dirt and trash on him while he prayed.
- They laughed at the weaker Muslims and beat them in public.

One day, when the Prophet ﷺ was praying near the Kaaba, someone placed a camel's stomach on his back while he was in sujood (prostration).

The Prophet ﷺ said:

"THEY ARE HARMING ME FOR CALLING THEM TO ALLAH."
— SIRAH IBN HISHAM

The Patience of Early Muslims

Many of the earliest Muslims were not rich or strong. They were slaves, servants, or poor people, but they were rich in iman (faith).

Let's learn about a few of them:

🔥 Bilal ibn Rabah (R.A.)

He was a black slave in Makkah. When he said, "Allah is One," his master tied him under the burning sun and placed a heavy stone on his chest. But Bilal never gave up.

He kept saying:

"AHAD! AHAD!"
(ALLAH IS ONE! ALLAH IS ONE!)
— SAHIH BUKHARI

His voice echoed through the barren mountains of 7th Century Makkah - strong and unwavering.

🔥Sumayyah bint Khayyat (R.A.)

She was one of the first women to accept Islam — and the first woman to die as a martyr. Her husband was Yasir (R.A.), and their son was Ammar (R.A.). All three of them were among the earliest Muslims.

But the idol-worshippers didn't like that. They tied them up and hurt them badly — just because they believed in Allah.

Still, they never gave up their faith. So the Prophet Muhammad ﷺ would pass by and say with love and sadness:

"Be patient, O family of Yasir! Your reward is Jannah (Paradise)."
— Mustadrak al-Hakim

🕊️ Hope Shines from Madinah

After many years of suffering, Allah gave the Prophet ﷺ and the Muslims a way out.

One night, the Prophet ﷺ told his companions:

"I have been shown the place of your migration… it is Yathrib (Madinah)."
— Sahih Bukhari

A Painful Goodbye

So one by one, the Muslims began to leave Makkah in secret. Some took camels, some walked, and some left behind everything they owned — only for the sake of Allah.

When the Prophet ﷺ left Makkah, he climbed a hill and looked back at the city he loved. With sadness in his heart, he said:

"By Allah, you are the most beloved land to me. Had your people not forced me out, I would never have left."
— Sunan al-Tirmidhi

That journey became known as the Hijrah — the greatest migration in Islamic history. It marked the beginning of a new chapter for the Muslims

🌟 Interesting Fact!

🕌 The first masjid (mosque) built by the Prophet ﷺ after Hijrah to Madinah was called Masjid Quba.

> The Prophet ﷺ used to visit it every Saturday.
> — Sahih Muslim

It was simple, but full of barakah (blessing)!

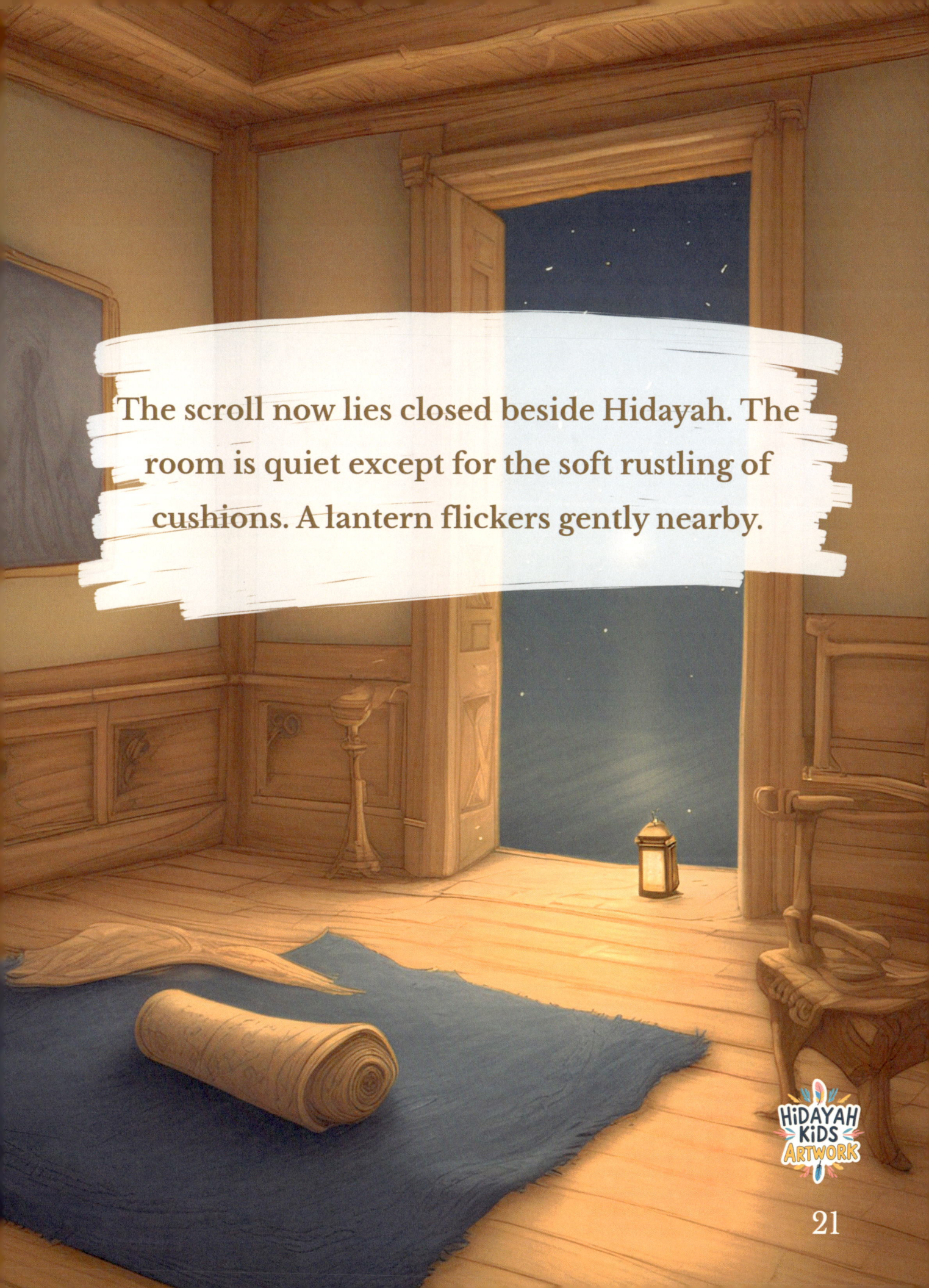

The scroll now lies closed beside Hidayah. The room is quiet except for the soft rustling of cushions. A lantern flickers gently nearby.

Emaan (wide-eyed, leaning back):
"That was... so hard to listen to. They were so brave — they left their homes for the sake of Allah!"

Shujā' (nodding slowly, unusually serious):
"Bilal (R.A.) didn't stop saying "Ahad! Ahad!" even with a giant stone on him. That's not just brave — that's mountain-heart brave."

Hidayah (smiling gently):
"Yes, Shujā. That's what real heroes do.
Today we learned that even when the world is against you, holding on to the truth makes you shine. Just like the early Muslims who even left their homes behind in Makkah."

Zarsha (bouncing slightly):
"Next story-y soon?"
(She meant: "Can we hear the next story soon?")

Hidayah (placing her hand on the scroll):
"Yes. But remember — it's not just a story. These were real people... with real hearts full of Iman. Let's keep our hearts strong too!"

 Glossary

Word	Meaning
Ahad	Arabic word for "One" — used for Allah
Hijrah	The journey from Makkah to Madinah
Idol	A statue that the people of Mecca use to wrongly worship as a god
Martyr	A person who dies for Allah's cause
Masjid	A place where Muslims pray (mosque)
Iman	Faith in Allah

CHAPTER 2
THE CALL TO BADR

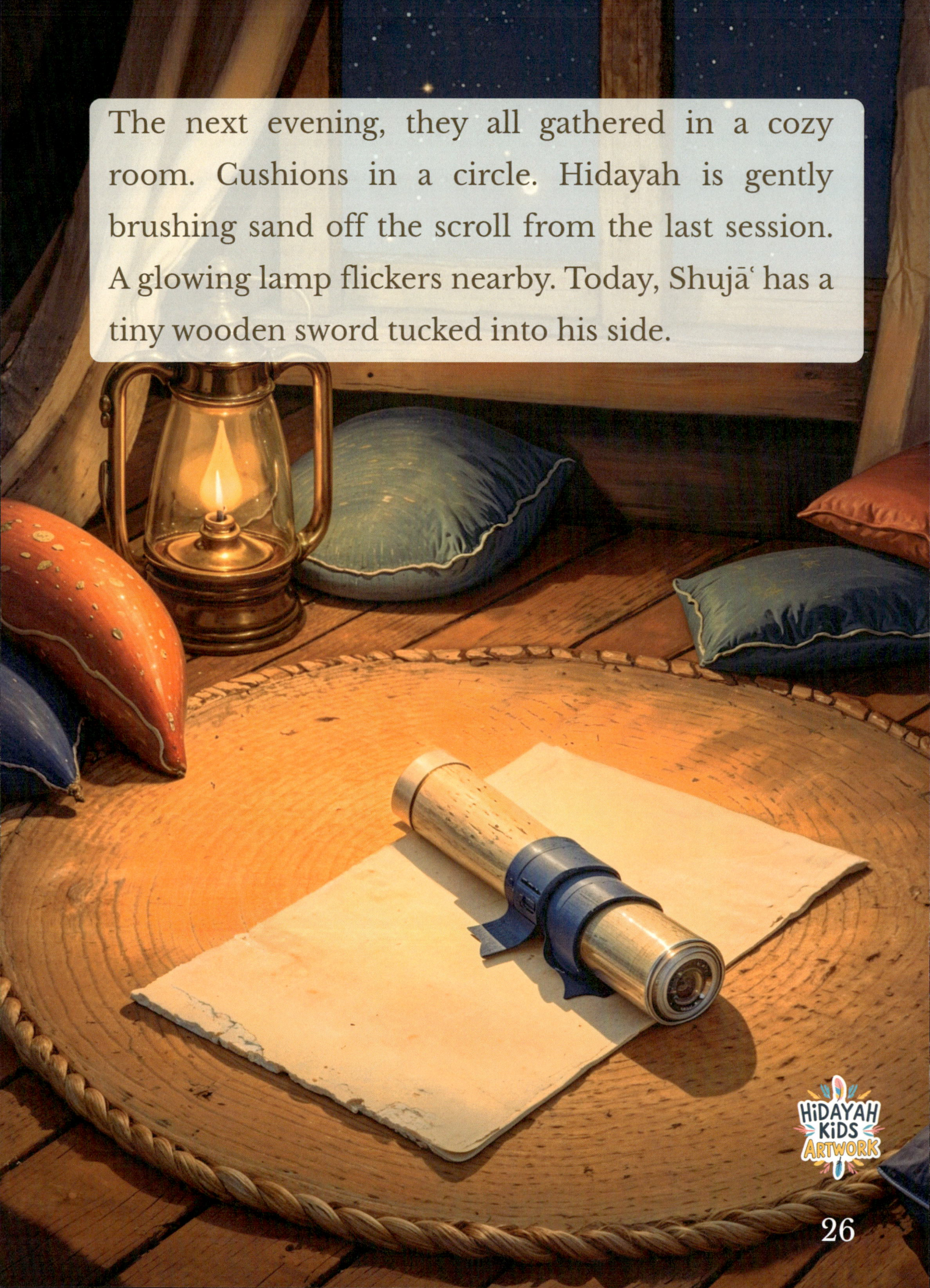

The next evening, they all gathered in a cozy room. Cushions in a circle. Hidayah is gently brushing sand off the scroll from the last session. A glowing lamp flickers nearby. Today, Shujāʿ has a tiny wooden sword tucked into his side.

Hidayah (retying the scroll with care):
"Alright team... it's time for what came next — the call to Badr. Do you know that the Muslims didn't even want to fight. They just wanted to get back what the disbelievers of Makkah stole."

Shujāʿ (holding a stick like a spear):
"And then came the mud... and the rain... and the camels slipping everywhere!"
(leans in, whispering)
"Please tell me one of the angels rode a camel."

Emaan (pointing at him):
"Shujāʿ, angels don't need camels! They have wings!"
Everyone smiles.

Zarsha (clapping with a toothy smile):
"Wingies! Zoom-zoom in the sky!"
(She meant: "Angels flying fast in the sky")

Hidayah (opening the scroll, eyes shining):
"This is the story of the first real battle... a day when dua and faith were stronger than swords. Let's begin.."

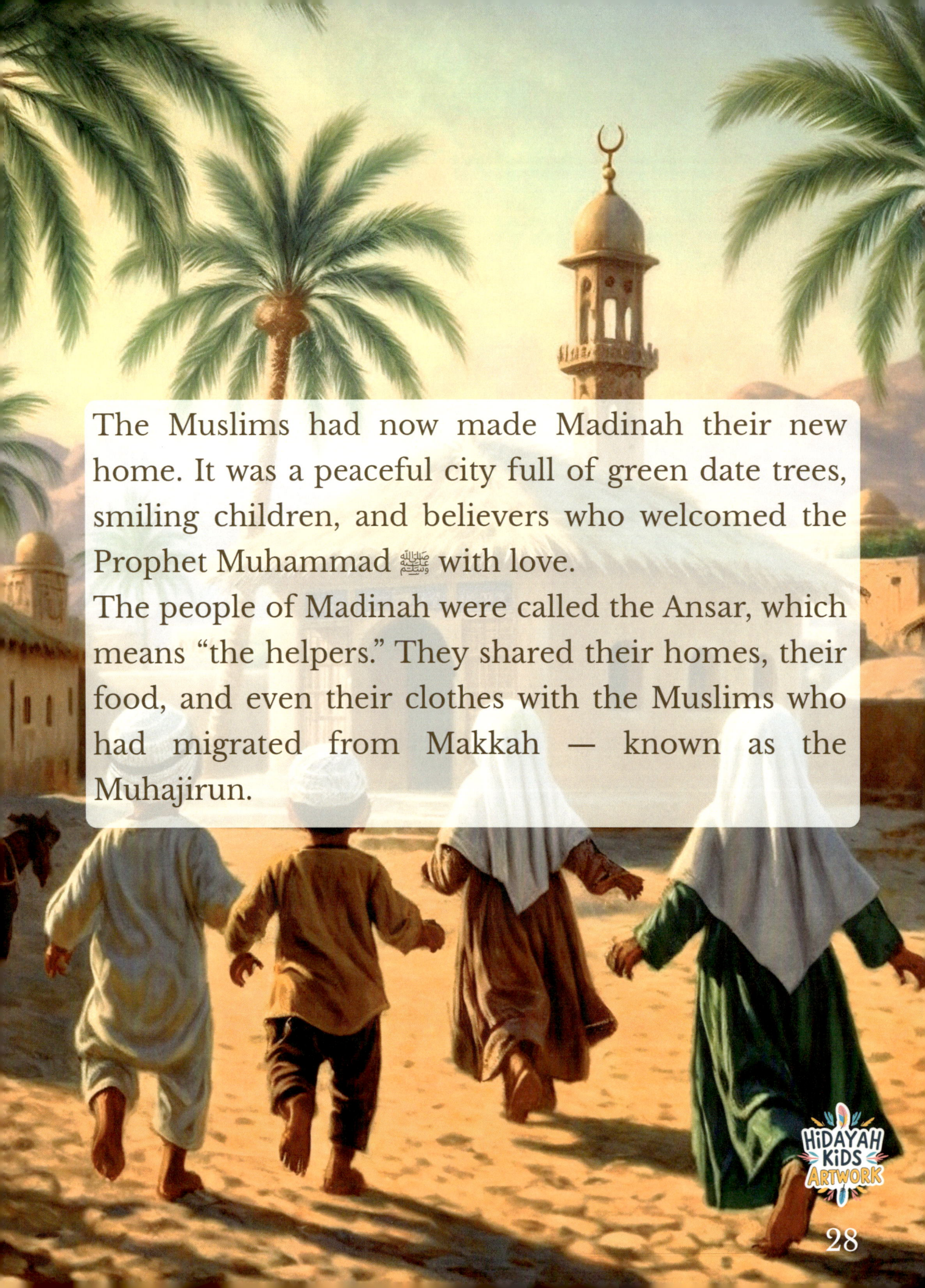

The Muslims had now made Madinah their new home. It was a peaceful city full of green date trees, smiling children, and believers who welcomed the Prophet Muhammad ﷺ with love.

The people of Madinah were called the Ansar, which means "the helpers." They shared their homes, their food, and even their clothes with the Muslims who had migrated from Makkah — known as the Muhajirun.

After moving to Madinah, the Muslims tried to live in peace. But the disbelievers were still angry. They had already taken the Muslims' homes and stolen their money. And now, they were planning something worse.

They hadn't forgotten the Muslims — and they didn't want Islam to grow.

Trouble was coming...!

🐪 The Disbelievers' Caravan

One day, the Prophet Muhammad ﷺ received news: a huge caravan of traders from Makkah — full of gold, food, and supplies — was traveling from Syria to Makkah, passing near Madinah.

It was led by Abu Sufyan R.A, one of the Quraysh leaders at that time – who later on accepted Islam many years after Badr and became a companion.

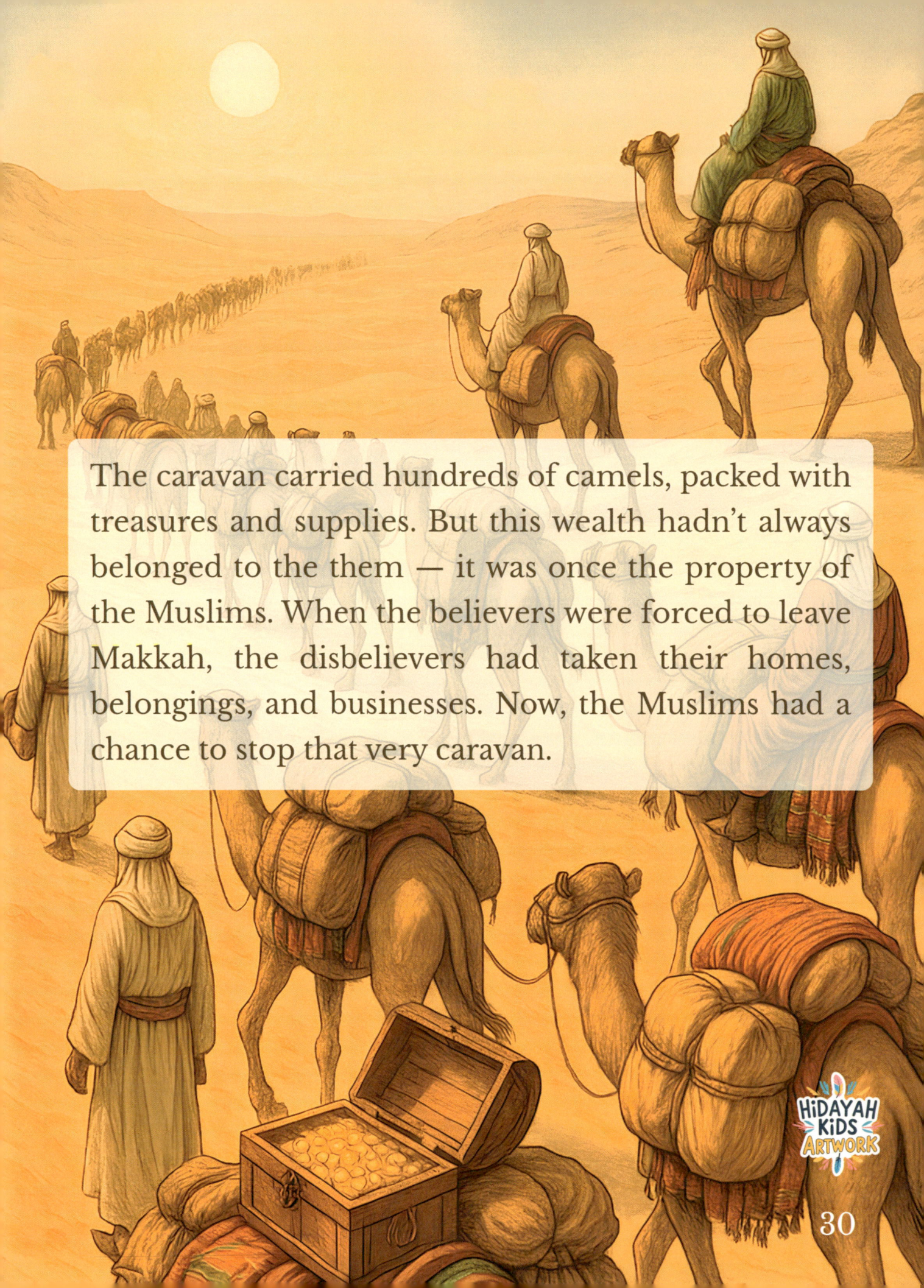

The caravan carried hundreds of camels, packed with treasures and supplies. But this wealth hadn't always belonged to the them — it was once the property of the Muslims. When the believers were forced to leave Makkah, the disbelievers had taken their homes, belongings, and businesses. Now, the Muslims had a chance to stop that very caravan.

Prophet Muhammad  said to his companions:

"This is the caravan of Quraysh, carrying their wealth. Go out to it; perhaps Allah will give it to you."
— Sunan Abi Dawood

But Abu Sufyan R.A heard about the Muslims too — and he quickly sent a rider back to Makkah to call for help.

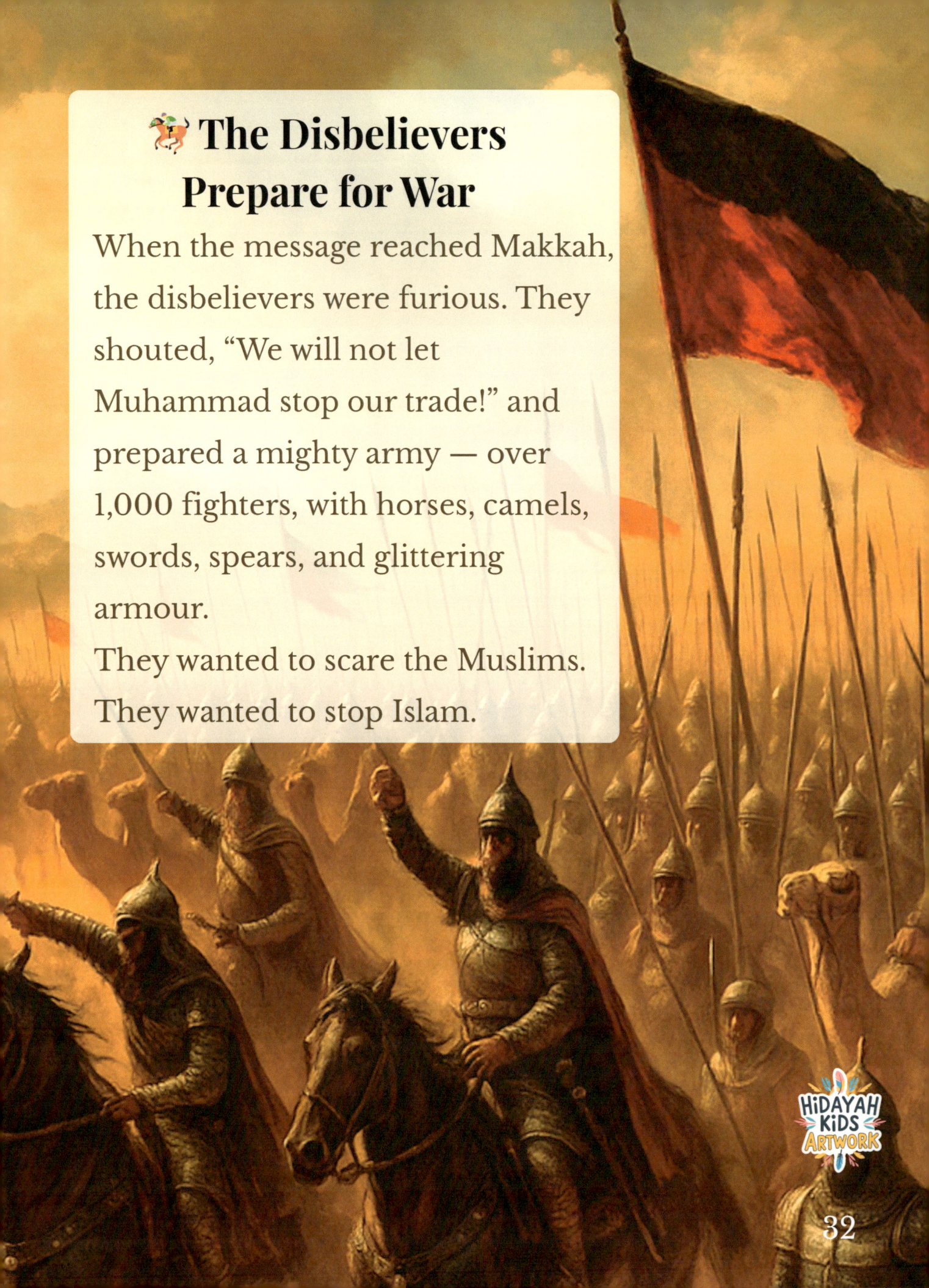

🐎 The Disbelievers Prepare for War

When the message reached Makkah, the disbelievers were furious. They shouted, "We will not let Muhammad stop our trade!" and prepared a mighty army — over 1,000 fighters, with horses, camels, swords, spears, and glittering armour.

They wanted to scare the Muslims. They wanted to stop Islam.

But the Muslims had only 313 people — many with no armour, no horses, and just a few weapons. Some had sticks. Others had broken swords. And yet, they had something the disbelievers didn't have:

Strong iman (faith), du'a of Prophet Muhammad ﷺ, and the promise of Allah's help.

Prophet Muhammad ﷺ gathered the companions and asked:

"Give me your opinion, O people!"

One by one, the companions stood up.

Abu Bakr (R.A.) said:

"Go where Allah commands you. We are with you!"

Umar ibn al-Khattab (R.A.) said:

"We will never say what Banī Israil said to Mūsā ('You and your Lord go fight — we'll stay here!'). We will fight beside you!"

But Prophet ﷺ wanted opinion from Ansar as well, because he was staying with them in Madina. Finally, a young leader from the Ansar named Sa'd ibn Mu'adh (R.A.) stood up. He said:

"If you cross the sea, we will follow you. We (Ansar) are patient in war (we won't run away), and truthful in loyalty."

— Sirah Ibn Hisham

Prophet Muhammad ﷺ smiled brightly and said:
"March forward and be glad. For Allah has promised me one of the two — the caravan or victory."
— Musnad Ahmad

🌧️ Rain and Dua

The Muslims camped near a place called Badr, a land between two rocky hills. There were wells of water nearby — which they protected wisely.

The night before the battle, many companions couldn't sleep. They prayed and remembered Allah. In a small tent, Prophet Muhammad ﷺ stood praying. He spent the whole night in sujood, begging Allah for help. His voice trembled as he raised his hands:

"O Allah, fulfill for me what You have promised me. . if this small group of Muslims is destroyed, You will not be worshipped on Earth after today."
— Sahih Muslim

He raised his hands so long that his shawl slipped off his shoulders. Abu Bakr (R.A.) came and gently placed the shawl back. He said:
"O Prophet of Allah ﷺ, Allah will never let you down."
— Sirah Ibn Hisham

Muslim Camp

That night, it rained gently — a gift from Allah.
The soft rain made the dusty ground firm under Muslim feet.

Enemy Camp

Whereas, the enemy camp became muddy and messy.

Interesting Facts!

- Near the battlefield of Badr, there is a small mountain known today as Jabal al-Mala'ikah (The Mountain of the Angels). Many locals in Madina believe this is the place where Allah sent angels to help the Muslim army.

- The number of angels initially sent by Allah to help the Muslims at Badr was 1,000 (Surah Al-Anfal 8:9). Then the Allah increased support to 3,000 and then 5,000, as a glad tiding (Surah Aal-Imran 3: 124-125) — Tafsir Ibn Kathir

The scroll is rolled back up. Hidayah places it gently on a shelf. Everyone is still quiet, thinking deeply about what they just heard. A soft wind brushes the curtain, letting in the cool night air. Outside, the stars twinkle above — as if the sky itself is remembering the story too.

If you had been there, you might have felt that the angels had ascended to listen the story of Prophet Muhammad ﷺ and his brave companions — their presence lingering like a whisper in the night.

Emaan (after a long silence, hugging her pretend sword close):
"So if we stay strong in our hearts... angels might come for us too?"

Hidayah (placing a hand on her chest):
"Allah will send help — comfort, courage, ideas, people and maybe angels — whatever we truly need."

Eman (her eyes glowing):
"When we go for our next 'Umrah, I shall ask Baba to take us to Badr. I really want to see that Mountain from where the angels ascended with my own eyes."

Shujāʿ (sitting up straight, proud):
"Fom now on, I shall make epic duʿa before every math test and scary moment!"
Everyone smiles — even Hidayah wipes a happy tear, the lantern light flickering around them.

Hidayah (quietly):
"Let's never forget — Allah's help is always near... for those who believe. Get some rest, brave ones. Because next time... the battle begins."

Glossary

Word	Meaning
Ansar	The Muslims of Madinah who helped Prophet Muhammad ﷺ
Badr	A place where the first and most important battle in Islam happened
Caravan	A group of people traveling with goods and camels
Dua	A prayer or supplication to Allah
Muhajirun	The Muslims who migrated from Makkah to Madinah

That night, they set up camp beneath the open sky. The stars sparkled brightly above, and a gentle breeze rustled the fabric of their canvas tent. Inside, a soft lantern glowed, casting warm shadows on the straw mat and cushions laid in a circle.

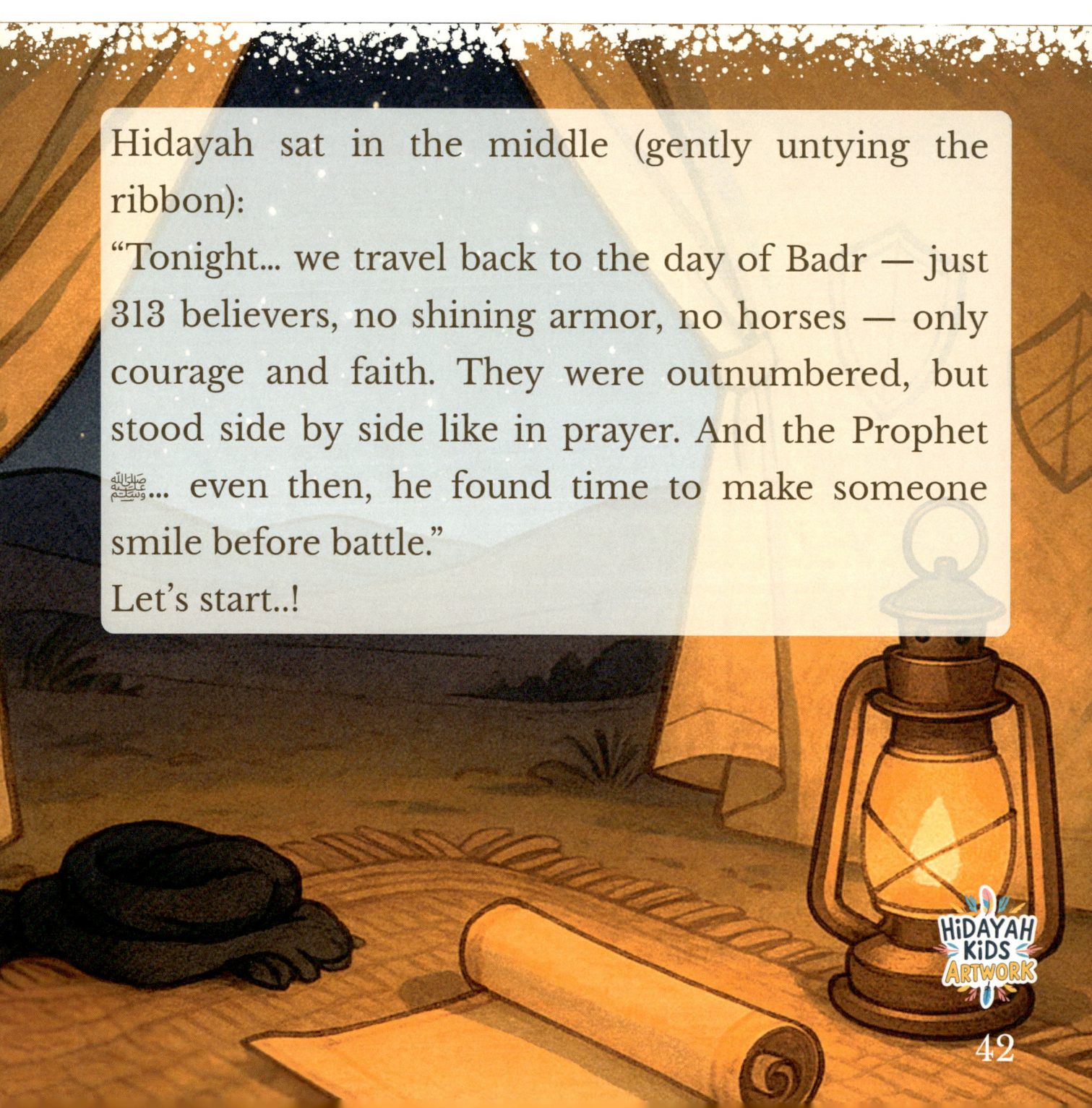

Hidayah sat in the middle (gently untying the ribbon):

"Tonight... we travel back to the day of Badr — just 313 believers, no shining armor, no horses — only courage and faith. They were outnumbered, but stood side by side like in prayer. And the Prophet ﷺ... even then, he found time to make someone smile before battle."

Let's start..!

The sun had just begun to rise over Badr, stretching golden light across the sand. The battlefield was quiet, but in the distance, clouds of dust floated in the air — the disbelievers' army was marching with over 1,000 soldiers, horses, and sharp swords. Their shields glittered in the sun.

But on the other side stood a much smaller group — only 313 believers who stood in rows, checking their swords, adjusting their belts.

The Muslims didn't have much:

Only 2 horses.

Around 70 camels (and they had to take turns riding).

A few swords, sticks, and broken shields.

No armor, no helmets, and some had no shoes at all!

Still, no one complained.

"We are not afraid! Allah is with us!" thought a young boy gripping a wooden stick.

🏹 Preparing for Battle

Prophet Muhammad ﷺ stood in front of the believers and arranged them in straight rows, just like in prayer. He held a small stick and gently moved companions into place.

He told them:

> "STAND IN STRAIGHT LINES, FOR THIS IS BETTER FOR YOUR UNITY AND STRENGTH."
> — MUSNAD AHMAD

One companion was standing slightly ahead. Prophet Muhammad ﷺ tapped his belly to bring him back in line. The man said:

> "O MESSENGER OF ALLAH ﷺ, YOU HAVE HURT ME!"

So the Prophet ﷺ smiled and let him poke him back with the stick. Instead, he hugged the Prophet ﷺ.

— SIRAH IBN HISHAM

Everyone laughed gently. Even in such a serious moment, the Prophet ﷺ was kind and just.

⚔️ The Battle Begins

The two sides stood still. Spears pointed. Banners waved. The disbelievers' army shouted loudly, stomping their feet to scare the Muslims. But the believers didn't shout back. Their hearts were steady. Their eyes looked forward. They weren't thinking about numbers. They were thinking about Allah.

Then, as the disbelievers charged forward and the earth rumbled beneath their feet, Prophet Muhammad ﷺ stepped out from the front of the Muslim line. Calm and fearless, he raised his hand, picked up a handful of dust, and faced the enemy with steady eyes...

He threw the dust toward them and said:

> "MAY THEIR FACES BE COVERED!"
> — SAHIH MUSLIM

A sudden gust of wind blew the dust straight into the disbeliever army's eyes.

💥 WHOOSH!

"Allahu Akbar!" shouted the Muslims. (Allah is the Greatest!)

And the battle began.

The air filled with the sound of clashing swords, galloping feet, and the cries of determination. Though the Muslims were outnumbered, they fought with courage and unity. Just as the two sides clashed and the battle grew fierce...

✨The Angels Are Coming!

Then something amazing happened.

Allah answered the Du'a of Prophet Muhammad ﷺ. These angels came down from the sky — fast and bright like lightning — but only the believers could see them.

They were not ordinary angels. They were warriors, carrying swords of light, riding white horses. They joined the Muslims in battle and made the hearts of the disbelievers shake with fear.

One companion said:

"I WAS ABOUT TO STRIKE A MAN, AND I HEARD A VOICE ABOVE ME SAYING, 'STRIKE HIM!' — AND THE MAN FELL BEFORE I COULD HIT HIM."
— SAHIH MUSLIM

The Muslims felt comfort in their hearts. Even though they were tired, hungry, and outnumbered, they stood strong. Some companions said they saw white turbans flying past.

Others heard voices from the sky calling.

"ADVANCE, O ARMY OF ALLAH!"
— TAFSIR IBN KATHIR ON SURAH AL-ANFAL 8:9–12

Ali ibn Abi Talib (R.A.), who was just a young man, fought bravely alongside others. He later said:

"VICTORY CAME FROM ABOVE THE SEVEN HEAVENS."
— AL-BIDAYAH WA AL-NIHAYAH BY IBN KATHIR

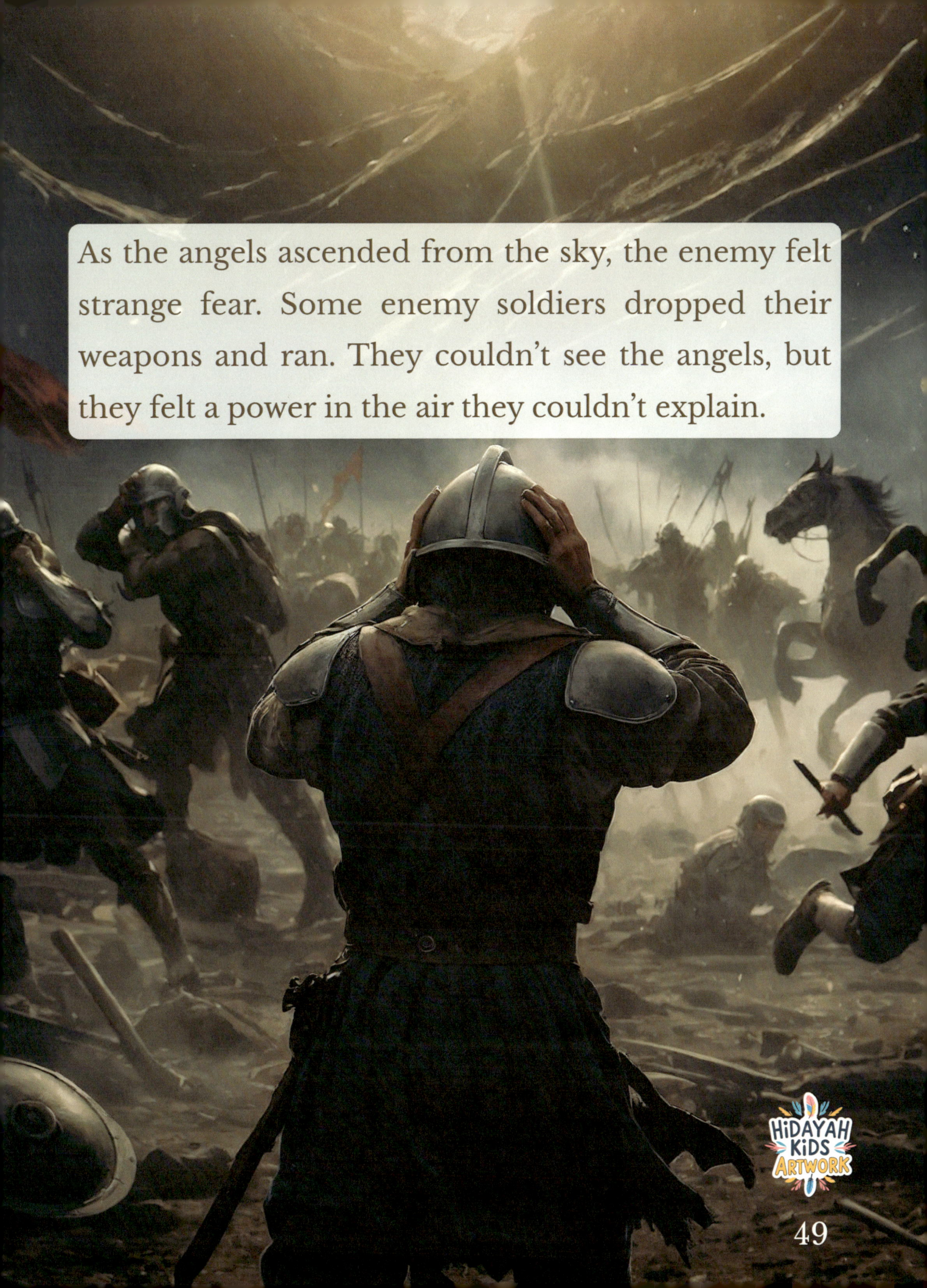

As the angels ascended from the sky, the enemy felt strange fear. Some enemy soldiers dropped their weapons and ran. They couldn't see the angels, but they felt a power in the air they couldn't explain.

⭐ Interesting Fact!

Some companions were only teenagers — like Umair ibn Abi Waqqas (R.A.), Mu'adh (R.A.), and Mu'awwidh (R.A.). They showed bravery far beyond their age!

The scroll is now rolled halfway. A soft light glows in the tent. Everyone sits quietly — the mood is thoughtful.

Emaan (eyes wide):
"We're talking real angels, right? Not in dreams — like actually there?"

Hidayah (nodding):
"Yes. The Muslims saw them, heard their voices, and felt peace in their hearts. Allah sent His help — just as He promised. This chapter teaches us something big — that true strength doesn't come from armor or numbers. It comes from faith, unity, and trusting Allah even when things look impossible."

Shujāʿ (adjusting his pretend turban, whispering):
"Next time we face a tough moment... remind me to look up. Just in case the angels are coming."
Everyone smiled.

Glossary

Word	Meaning
Allahu Akbar	Arabic phrase meaning "Allah is the Greatest"
Dua	A prayer or supplication to Allah
Reinforce	To give more strength or support
Sujood	Prostration during prayer (putting forehead on the ground)
Iman	Faith in Allah

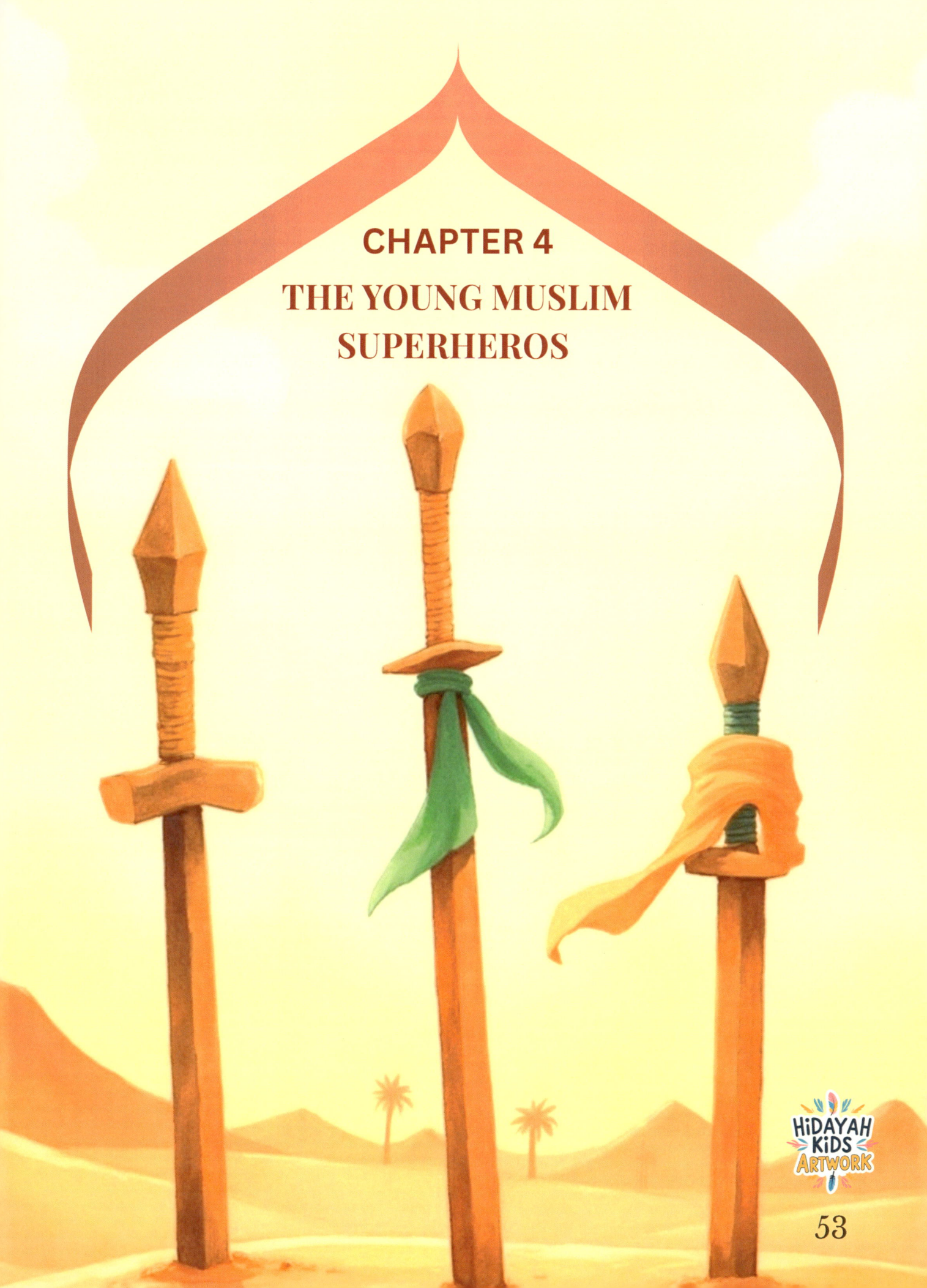

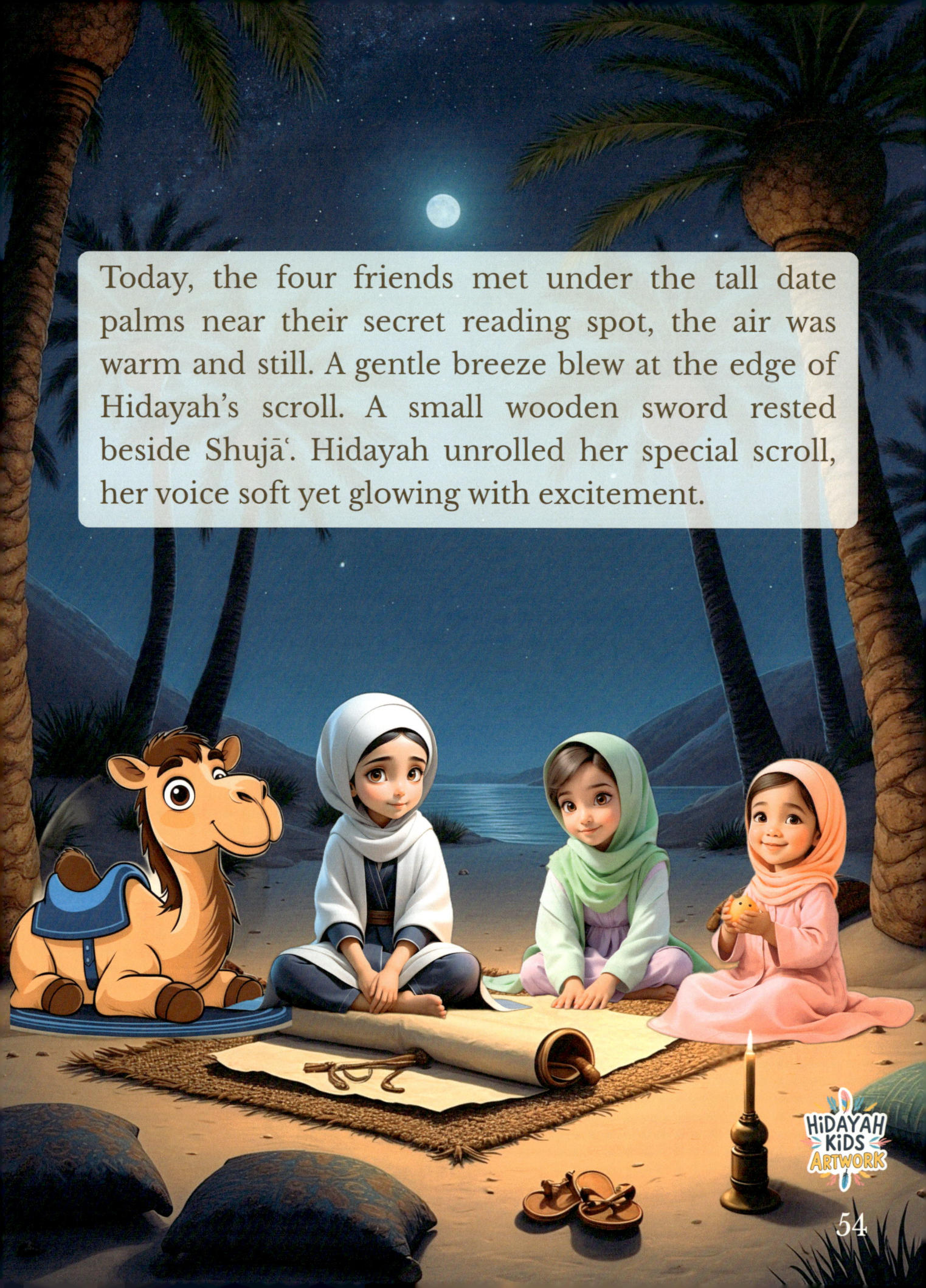

Today, the four friends met under the tall date palms near their secret reading spot, the air was warm and still. A gentle breeze blew at the edge of Hidayah's scroll. A small wooden sword rested beside Shujāʿ. Hidayah unrolled her special scroll, her voice soft yet glowing with excitement.

Hidayah (smiling):

"Alright... are you ready for the most amazing superhero stories ever told? Not the kind with flying or fire-blasting or magical powers. These heroes didn't wear capes... or swing from webs. They weren't cartoons. They were real. Real heroes — small in size, but mighty in faith."

She paused, letting the words settle like golden dust in the air.

"They stood beside the Prophet Muhammad ﷺ at the Battle of Badr... even when the odds were against them. They didn't save imaginary cities — they stood to defend the truth. They didn't have superpowers — They had something far stronger: Iman.

Faith was their shield. Love for Allah and His Messenger ﷺ was their strength."

Her voice dropped to a whisper.
"Their names may not be in comic books... But their courage is written in the skies above Badr."

She looked up with a soft smile.
"So now... let's meet the real superheroes. With real hearts. Cooler than laser eyes, right?"

Hidayah turned the scroll slowly.
"The first story is about a young companion who couldn't stay behind — even when he was told he was too small to fight.
His name was Umair ibn Abi Waqqas (R.A.) — and he was just 16 years old. Want to hear what he did?"
They all nodded quietly. The scroll opened fully...And the story began.

The Youngest Warrior – Umair ibn Abi Waqqas (R.A.)

Near the back of the Muslim army, a small boy stood quietly, trying not to be noticed. His name was Umair ibn Abi Waqqas (R.A.) — the younger brother of Sa'd ibn Abi Waqqas (R.A.). He was only about 16 years old, but his heart beat with the courage of someone far older.

A few days earlier, just before the journey to Badr, Umair (R.A.) approached the Prophet Muhammad ﷺ, asking for permission to join the army.

He stood before the Prophet Muhammad ﷺ, with his voice full of hope and fire and said:

"O Messenger of Allah ﷺ, let me fight alongside you."

The Prophet ﷺ looked at him with kindness. His face was youthful. His sword was too big. His armor didn't quite fit. The Prophet ﷺ gently turned him away as he was still too young.

Umair's (R.A.) heart sank. His eyes filled with tears that he tried hard to hide. He wanted nothing more than to defend Islam, to stand beside the Prophet ﷺ, and to prove his love for Allah.

When the Prophet PBUH saw the tears in his eyes and felt the sincerity in his heart, he smiled — a smile full of mercy and pride. He then allowed Umair (R.A.) to join the army.

When the soldiers began preparing to march toward Badr, Umair (R.A.) proudly took his place among them. His armor still didn't sit right. His sword dragged slightly behind him. But he didn't care. He wasn't thinking about his size — he was thinking about Jannah.

And so, this young boy with a trembling heart stood beside grown men, ready to face an army three times their size.

When the battle began, Umair (R.A.) rushed forward with the others.
The sound of swords and shouts filled the air.
Dust rose. Arrows flew. Swords clashed.

💥 THUMP! THUMP!

And the young warrior who had once been turned away... now stood shoulder to shoulder with the bravest of the brave.

Umair ibn Abi Waqqas (R.A.) fought bravely that day.
He didn't fight for fame.
He didn't speak grand words.
But his actions wrote his name in history — the young boy who wouldn't stay behind when the truth was calling.

He fought with everything he had.
And that day, he fell in battle — a shaheed, one of the youngest martyrs of Badr.
And the shuhadā' of Badr... their names were written by the angels, and their place in Jannah was promised — for they stood on a day when the truth faced its first great test.

— Sirah Ibn Hisham & Maghazi al-Waqidi

As the scroll ended, a quiet hush filled the air. The stars above twinkled softly. Even the wind seemed to pause.
Emaan sat with her hands around her knees, eyes wide.

Zarsha (softly):
"He was just a boy... but he didn't want to be left behind."
 (She looked at her hands, thinking.)
 "He didn't wait to grow taller. He just... went."

Shuja the baby camel (blinking slowly under the starlight, lifted his head in soft voice):
"Wow.. He didn't wait for tomorrow... He gave Allah his today"
The others grew quiet again.

Hidayah (gently rolling up the scroll, her voice calm but full of emotion):
"Umair (R.A.) wasn't strong or tall as compared to enemy soldiers. But his heart... it was bigger than fear. Bravery isn't about size —
It's about what you're ready to leave behind for Allah. And that makes him one of the youngest, bravest heroes of all."

🌟 The Two Lion Cubs – Mu'adh and Mu'awwidh (R.A.)

Hidayah (turning the scroll):
"Now... it's time for the second story."
(She looks up, her voice gaining strength.)

"These next two Muslim superheroes were like lion cubs — small in size but fierce in faith. Just 13 or 14 years old, yet their eyes locked on the scariest enemy in Makkah... and they didn't stop until justice was done.

Were they scared? Not for a moment. Their hearts beat with courage — so loudly, their story still echoes across the sands of Badr.

Their names? Muʿadh ibn ʿAmr (R.A.) and Muʿawwidh ibn al-Ḥārith (R.A.). Two young lions... who walked into battle like warriors."

The children leaned in — silent, still, and ready to witness bravery beyond imagination.

The wind whispered across the battlefield.

In the middle of the Muslim camp stood two small boys, side by side, gripping their short swords tightly.

They were Mu'adh ibn 'Amr (R.A.) and Mu'awwidh ibn al Harith (R.A.) — both about 13 or 14 years old.

They weren't big. They weren't loud. But they had something that the disbelievers didn't have:

🔥 Faith.

They had been waiting for this day.

"Do you see him yet?" Mu'awwidh (R.A.) whispered.

"No. But we will," replied Mu'adh (R.A.).

Their eyes scanned the disbelievers' army.

A companion nearby heard them and asked:

"Who are you two looking for?"

The boys looked up and said with firm voices:

"Abu Jahl. The one who hurt Prophet Muhammad ﷺ in Makkah."

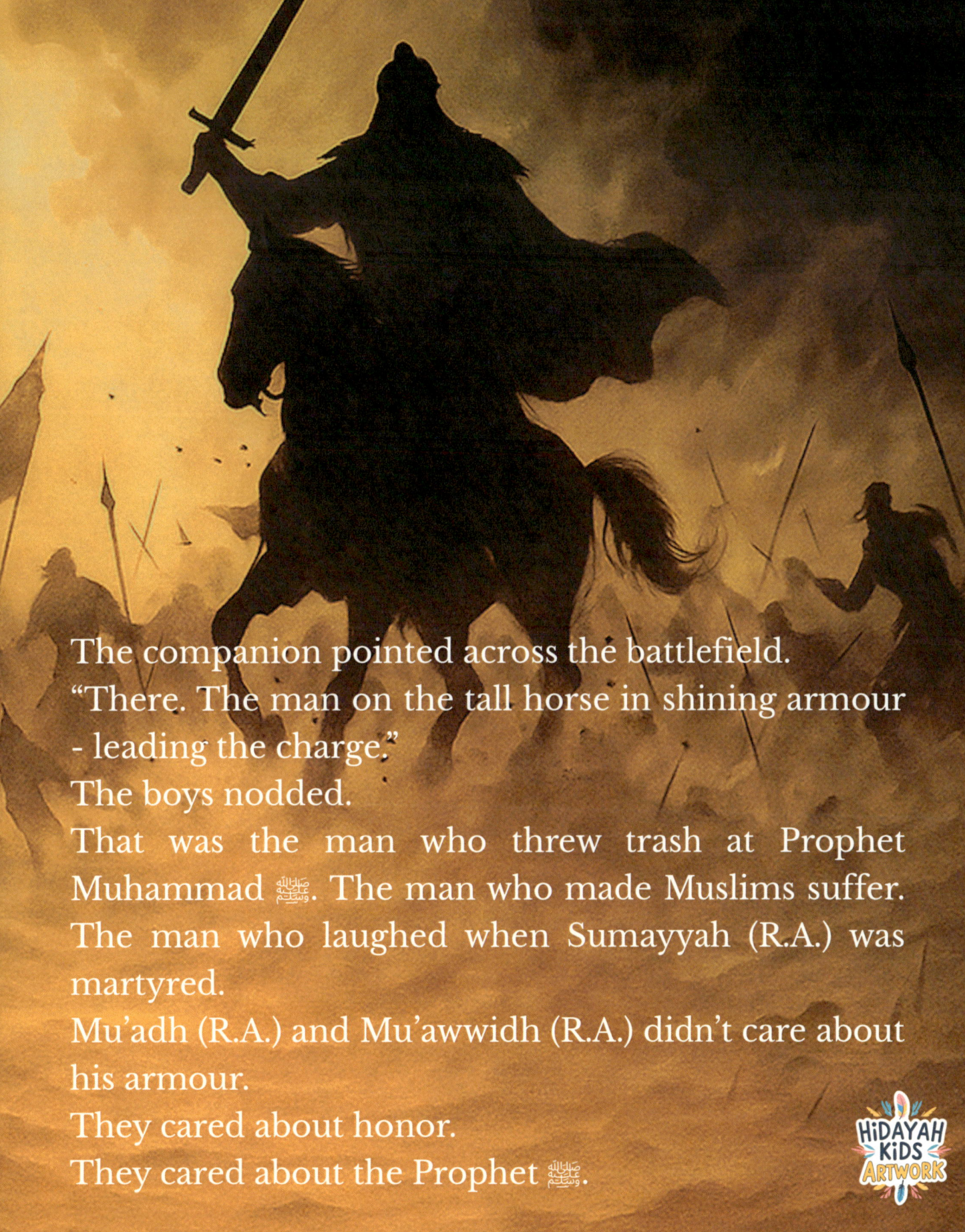

The companion pointed across the battlefield.
"There. The man on the tall horse in shining armour - leading the charge."
The boys nodded.
That was the man who threw trash at Prophet Muhammad ﷺ. The man who made Muslims suffer. The man who laughed when Sumayyah (R.A.) was martyred.
Mu'adh (R.A.) and Mu'awwidh (R.A.) didn't care about his armour.
They cared about honor.
They cared about the Prophet ﷺ.

When the battle began, they moved like two shadows across the sand.

💥 WHOOSH!

They ran between horses and camels, ducking under swinging swords, dodging spears, slipping past enemy lines.

Their hearts pounded. Their fingers tightened on their swords.

And then they saw him — Abu Jahl, yelling orders, standing proud.

The boys didn't wait.

💥 SLASH!

💥 STRIKE!

Their swords hit hard. They struck Abu Jahl's legs and brought him down from his horse. He screamed and fell — shocked that two boys could bring him to the ground.

He lay injured, shouting in pain. Later, Abdullah ibn Mas'ud (R.A.) came and ended it. But it was Mu'adh (R.A.) and Mu'awwidh (R.A.) who opened the door to justice.

Their bravery was remembered by the companions — two boys whose hearts burned for justice.

And that's who they were.

Two lion cubs. Young. But fearless.

The children sat quietly, their eyes wide, as if they had just returned from the battlefield of Badr themselves. For a moment, no one moved.

Shujāʿ (eyes shining):
"So... they weren't the biggest or the strongest... but they still brought down the scariest man in Makkah?"

Hidayah (voice soft, yet full of meaning):
"Now you know what makes a real hero? It's not a big sword. Or a loud voice. It's a big heart — one that loves truth more than it fears anything else."

Emaan (nodding slowly):
"Even if I'm small... I can still do something big?"

Hidayah (gently):
"Exactly. Like standing up for what's right. Helping someone. Or just saying the truth — even when it's hard. That's superhero stuff too..."

The Young Companion Who Threw His Dates – Umair ibn al-Ḥammām (R.A.)

The group was still thinking about the brave lion cubs from the last story.

Hidayah gently turns the scroll, the soft evening light flickering across its edges. She looks up, her voice steady and glowing with awe.

Hidayah:
"Now... it's time for the third story.
But this one isn't about someone who sneaked in... or someone who had a sword.
It's about a young and energetic companion who threw away his dates... just to get to Jannah faster.
His name was Umair ibn al-Ḥammām (R.A.) — and he was an energetic young man.

Ready to hear what he did?"
They all nodded quietly. The scroll opened fully...
And the story began.

As the army gathered near the battlefield of Badr, a soft desert wind curled through the valley. The sand trembled faintly beneath thousands of footsteps — Quraysh horses on one side, the humble believers on the other.

Prophet Muhammad ﷺ walked among the companions, looking at their faces one by one. The Muslim army stood quietly. Their shields were rough. Their swords were few. Dust clung to their faces. But their hearts were steady.

He reminded the companions that whoever stood firm, remained patient, and faced the enemy without turning back — Allah had promised him Paradise.

— Sahih Muslim

His words floated through the air like sparks. Some gasped. Others stood taller.

And one companion — Umair ibn al-Ḥammām (R.A.), a young warrior from the Ansār — stood frozen, dates in his hand, heart racing. He had only taken a few out to eat. But now, his eyes locked on the Prophet ﷺ, wide with wonder. Paradise? Just like that?

He stepped forward and asked:

"O Messenger of Allah, is there nothing between me and Paradise except to be killed by them (while I fight for justice)?"

The Prophet ﷺ replied simply:
"No."

That was all Umair needed to hear.

He looked down at the sticky dates in his palm. Sweet, soft, and comforting. He held them tightly... then loosened his grip.

His fingers opened. The dates slipped to the ground.

"If I live until I eat all of them, that's too long!"

— Sahih Muslim

He sprinted forward — dust flying behind him, sword swinging at his side, lips whispering:

"Allahu Akbar... Allahu Akbar..."

💥 THUMP! THUMP!

The valley erupted in thunder.

The Quraysh of Mecca came crashing down with their horses, flags, and roars. Swords clashed like lightning. Arrows hissed through the sky like angry wind.

Umair (R.A.) didn't slow down.
He ran through the chaos with fire in his chest and Jannah in his sight.
And that day — he fell as a shaheed.
He didn't wait.
He didn't fear.
He didn't finish his dates.
He raced toward Paradise... with the words of the Prophet ﷺ still ringing in his ears.

He didn't just believe in Jannah.
He rushed toward it — without hesitation, without a bite more, without ever looking back.

— Sahih Muslim

The scroll rested gently in Hidayah's lap. A quiet stillness wrapped around them like a warm blanket. The date palms above swayed slowly, their leaves whispering secrets to the wind.
The stars above blinked softly — as if they, too, remembered Umair (R.A.)

Zarsha (looking at her half-eaten date, voice soft and wide-eyed):
"He really gave it up… just like that?"
(She held the date tighter, as if understanding its meaning for the first time.)

Emaan (nodding, eyes shining):
"Because to him… Jannah was sweeter than anything else."
(Her words settled in the air like a quiet echo.)

Hidayah (gently rolling up the scroll, her voice thoughtful and clear):
"Umair (R.A.) didn't wait to finish his dates. He knew Jannah was just one step away — and he didn't want to be late. Sometimes, we think we have time…and we can do good deeds later. But the people who truly love Allah, run towards him — right away."

🌟 The Voice of Courage – Barrah bint Abdul Muttalib (R.A.)

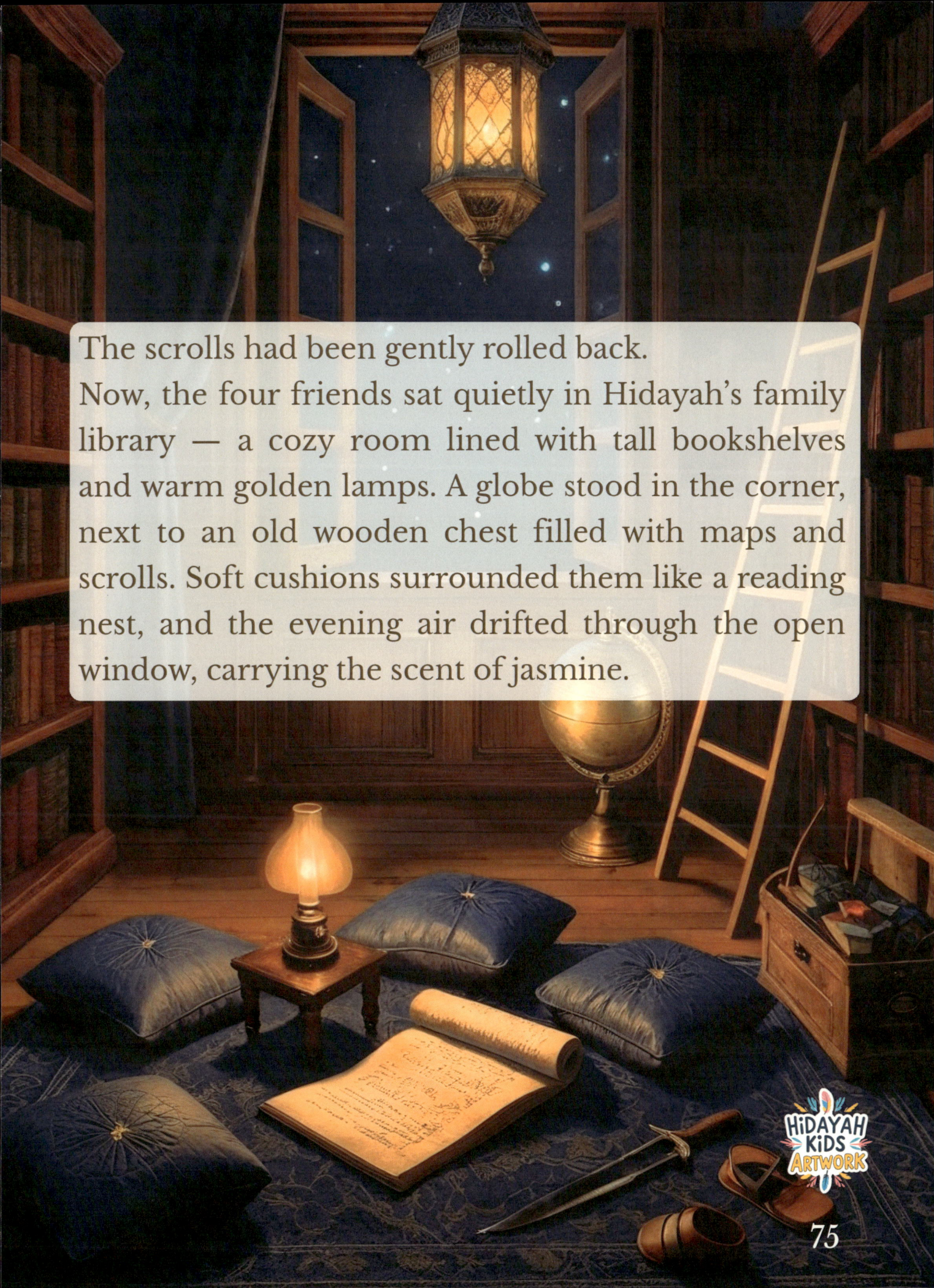

The scrolls had been gently rolled back.
Now, the four friends sat quietly in Hidayah's family library — a cozy room lined with tall bookshelves and warm golden lamps. A globe stood in the corner, next to an old wooden chest filled with maps and scrolls. Soft cushions surrounded them like a reading nest, and the evening air drifted through the open window, carrying the scent of jasmine.

Hidayah (gently, but with a clear voice):
"Now... it's time for the fourth story. But this one is a little different. It's not about the battlefield of Badr... or swords... or even arrows. It's about the heroes behind the battlefield — the ones who didn't go to fight... but whose words and du'as were like shields sent from far away.

This story takes us to Madinah... to the women and children who stayed behind. And one of them... was the Prophet's ﷺ own aunt.

She didn't wear armour. She didn't carry a sword. But her courage was as loud as thunder — and as soft as a mother's hand."

Far away from the battlefield of Badr, in the peaceful city of Madinah, the streets were quiet.

The men had left.

The army had marched.

But the hearts of those who stayed behind beat just as strongly as those standing on the battlefield.

Madinah was unusually quiet that morning.

The dust hadn't settled from the army's departure. Only the footprints of sandals and the scent of warm dates remained. In the alleys and courtyards, small groups of women gathered — their hands weaving, grinding, sweeping — but their hearts had followed the men far into the desert.

Some sat near the Prophet's mosque. Others shaded themselves beneath date trees. Their eyes often drifted toward the road that led out of the city... as if hoping to see something. Or someone.

A soft murmur passed between them.

The disbelievers are so many...

They have armour. Our sons are too young...

What if they never returned?

And then, as though the wind itself paused to listen — someone walked forward.

She wasn't carrying a sword.

She wore no armour.

But she carried something deeper.

Barrah bint 'Abdul Muṭṭalib (R.A.), the Prophet's ﷺ aunt, moved through the streets of Madinah like a steady flame. Her eyes calm. Her steps firm. There was no fear in her voice — only trust.

She reminded the people that armies do not decide victory — Allah does. That the people of truth had never been many, but they had always been strong. And that strength... begins with the heart.

She sat beside a mother who had wrapped herself in silence since her son left for Badr. His sandals still sat near the door, dusty but waiting. The mother held them like they might speak.

She visited more homes. Some women had sent their husbands, others their brothers or sons — some just boys. One mother whispered that her son was only sixteen.

But her presence was like a shield — not made of iron, but of faith. She spoke of what really mattered: not age, not numbers, not swords... but sincerity. That Allah sees the hearts, not the armour.

Her voice wasn't loud.

But it spread — like light under a door.

And it carried. Across rooms. Across rooftops. Across Madinah.

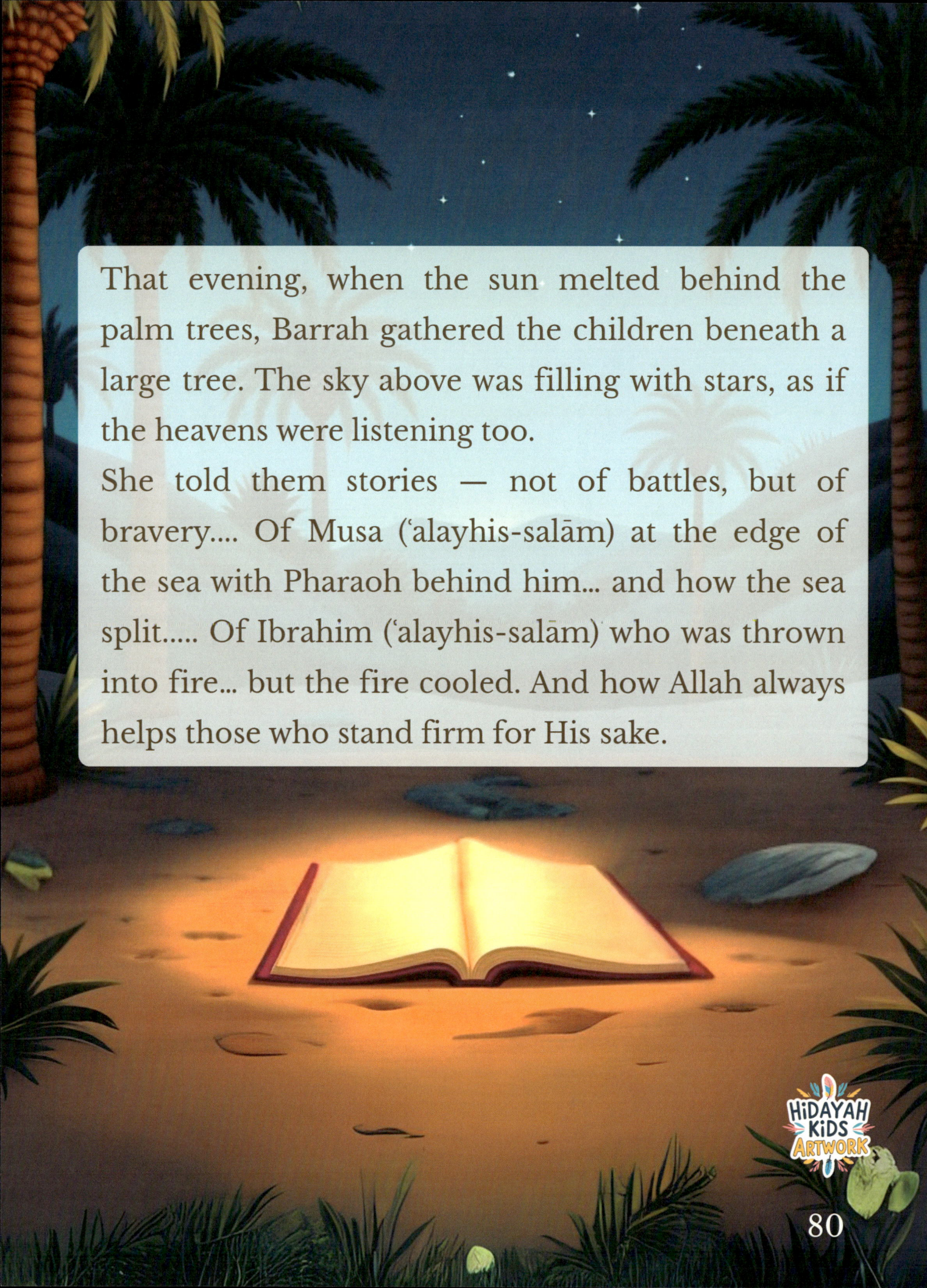

That evening, when the sun melted behind the palm trees, Barrah gathered the children beneath a large tree. The sky above was filling with stars, as if the heavens were listening too.

She told them stories — not of battles, but of bravery.... Of Musa ('alayhis-salām) at the edge of the sea with Pharaoh behind him... and how the sea split..... Of Ibrahim ('alayhis-salām) who was thrown into fire... but the fire cooled. And how Allah always helps those who stand firm for His sake.

Then she looked at them — little eyes, little hands, and hearts growing bigger with every word.

She told them that one day, they too would stand strong. Not just with swords. But with truth. With manners. With duʿā. And that sometimes, real courage begins not in the battlefield... but in the courtyard, when you choose trust over fear.

That night, as the children drifted to sleep, Madinah felt different. Lighter. Calmer.

The men had gone to Badr.

But the women — and their duʿās — had not been left behind.

Note for the Parents and Educators:

This story presents a narrative retelling of Barrah bint ʿAbdul Muṭṭalib's (R.A.) historical role in Madinah during the Battle of Badr. While no direct quotes are recorded from her, her presence, leadership, and unwavering trust in Allah are documented in:
– Tabaqat Ibn Saʿd, and
– Sirah Ibn Hisham

They all sat quietly for a moment, imagining the streets of Madinah… and the brave woman whose voice still echoed through time — not because she shouted, but because she believed.

Emaan (eyes wide with wonder):
"She didn't fight… but she still became a hero?"

Zarsha (nodding firmly):
"Even her duʿā flew like arrows!"

Hidayah (softly, her voice full of respect):
"Barrah showed us that courage isn't always loud. It doesn't always hold a sword.
Sometimes, it's a voice raised in truth… or a duʿā whispered with tears.
Real strength is when you use what you have — your voice, your kindness, your faith — to help others stand taller."

🌟 The Brother Who Fought with Both Hands and Heart – Sa'd ibn Abi Waqqas (R.A.)

Hidayah now reached for the final scroll, her fingers moving with care. She unrolled it slowly. Her voice, when it came, was calm... but carried a quiet weight.

"This one... is the final story from Badr.

But it's not just about swords or shields... It's about love. And pain.

It's about standing for what's right — even when your heart is breaking."

She paused, then looked at her sisters and Shujāʿ.

"It's about two brothers... Saʿd ibn Abi Waqqas (R.A.) and his younger brother Umair (R.A.).

One stood beside the Prophet ﷺ with a bow in his hand.

The other snuck into the army... just to get a chance at Jannah - a story which we have already read."

She gently tapped the edge of the scroll.

Everyone leaned in. The story began.

The wind blew gently over the desert of Badr, lifting swirls of sand into the air. The battlefield was ready, and so was Sa'd ibn Abi Waqqas (R.A.). He stood tall, his eyes fixed on the enemy line. In his hand, he held a bow — strong, curved, and well-worn. On his back was a quiver full of arrows.

But in his heart, he carried something heavier.

His younger brother, Umair ibn Abi Waqqas (R.A.), had snuck into the army. Sa'd (R.A.) had tried to stop him. Umair (R.A.) was only 16 — too young, too small. But too full of faith to be left behind.

— Sirah Ibn Hisham

Sa'd (R.A.) remembered the tears in Umair (R.A.s') eyes, the quiet way he had slipped into the back row. And now, they stood in the same battle — one beside the Prophet ﷺ, one hidden among the warriors.

When the enemy army began to move forward, Sa'd (R.A) stepped forward, looked into the distance... and became the first person in Islam to shoot an arrow in battle.

— Sahih al-Bukhari

He was so special that Prophet ﷺ later honored him (during the battle of Uhud) with a special phrase used only for a few companions:

"Shoot, O Sa'd! May my parents be sacrificed for you!"

Sahih Muslim

This was a special honor. The Prophet ﷺ only said this for a few companions in all of history.

Sa'd (R.A.) didn't just shoot arrows — he fought with calm strength. He stood near Prophet Muhammad's ﷺ tent and protected him when the enemy tried to break through.

– Tabaqāt Ibn Sa'd

Each time Sa'd fired an arrow, the Prophet ﷺ raised his hands and made Dua for him.

"O Allah, make Sa'd's aim true."
– Musnad Ahmad

Later, as the sun began to lower, Sa'd (R.A.) stood on the dusty ground, tired but unshaken.
Then he saw someone lying still.
It was his brother Umair (R.A.) — martyred at Badr, just as he had hoped.

Sa'd (R.A.) knelt beside him. He didn't cry loudly. But his heart remembered his brother.

He stood, pulled another arrow from his quiver, and whispered:
"This one's for you, Umair."
💥 THWACK!

Another arrow flew.
Another memory made.

— Seerah Ibn Hisham, &
— Maghazi al-Waqidi

Could You Be Like Sa'd (R.A.)?

He protected his Prophet .

He led by example.

And he fought with his hands... but also with his love.

"True warriors fight not with anger... but with purpose."

The night had gently settled over their little reading spot. A silver moonlight shimmered across, casting soft shadows as the scroll lay beside them.

Emaan (wiping her tears, voice soft):
"Saʿd (R.A.) fought and stayed close to the Prophet ﷺ. That's double the bravery."

Hidayah (looking down at the scroll, then raising her eyes slowly):
"Yes... but do you know what's even harder than being brave in battle? It's staying strong when your heart feels broken. Fighting for the truth while carrying the pain of loss. That's the courage Saʿd (R.A.) showed.."

Shujāʿ (thoughtfully):
"He stood for the truth — even after he lost someone he loved. He didn't stop because he was hurting — he kept going because he knew his brother would've wanted him to"

Zarsha (yawning, rubbing her eyes):
"That was my favrite favrit chapter..."
(She meant: "favorite")

91

Emaan (leaning back with a smile):
"Mine too. It showed that even kids — even we — can be superheroes."

Shujāʿ (stretching proudly):
"I don't need super strength. I've got super sincerity!"

But then he tripped over his foot and fell with a soft "oomph," making everyone smile.

Hidayah (speaking gently as she rolled up the scroll):

"Whether armed or not, having Iman and using it for truth makes you a hero in Allah's eyes"

They looked at each other and quietly nodded — hearts full, eyes shining with new dreams.

Emaan (eyes wide, almost whispering):
"So... what happened next? Did the Muslims... actually win the battle?"

Hidayah (smiling and rolling the scroll back):

"Well, that's for the final chapter, a story of angels and answered prayers. But for tonight, let's rest our hearts with Saʿd (R.A.) and Umair (R.A.)."

YOUNG MUSLIM HEROES OF BADR

At least five companions under the age of 18 fought at the Battle of Badr — and they weren't hiding in the back! They stood in the front rows — not because of size, but because of sincerity, skills, and their love for Allah ﷻ and the Prophet ﷺ.

- Umair ibn Abī Waqqās (R.A.), only about 16 years old, slipped into the army quietly — and became one of the youngest martyrs of Badr.
- Muʿadh (R.A.) & Muʿawwidh (R.A.) - though very young (13 or 14), struck boldly against Abu Jahl in the heat of battle.
- Umair ibn al-Ḥammām (R.A.) - was the young companion who threw his dates and rushed to Jannah.
- Saʿd ibn Abi Waqqas (R.A.) - was the first to shoot an arrow in the battle — and the Prophet ﷺ personally made duʿa for his accuracy.

These weren't fantasy superheroes.
They were real.

📚 Glossary

Word	Meaning
Hadith	A saying or action of Prophet Muhammad ﷺ that was recorded and passed down.
Jannah	Paradise — the most beautiful place promised by Allah ﷻ to the believers.
Lion cubs	A symbol for brave youth — Mu'adh and Mu'awwidh (R.A.).
Martyr	Another word for shaheed — someone who dies while standing up for the truth.
Muslim Superhero	Someone who uses courage, faith, and sincerity to help others and please Allah ﷻ.

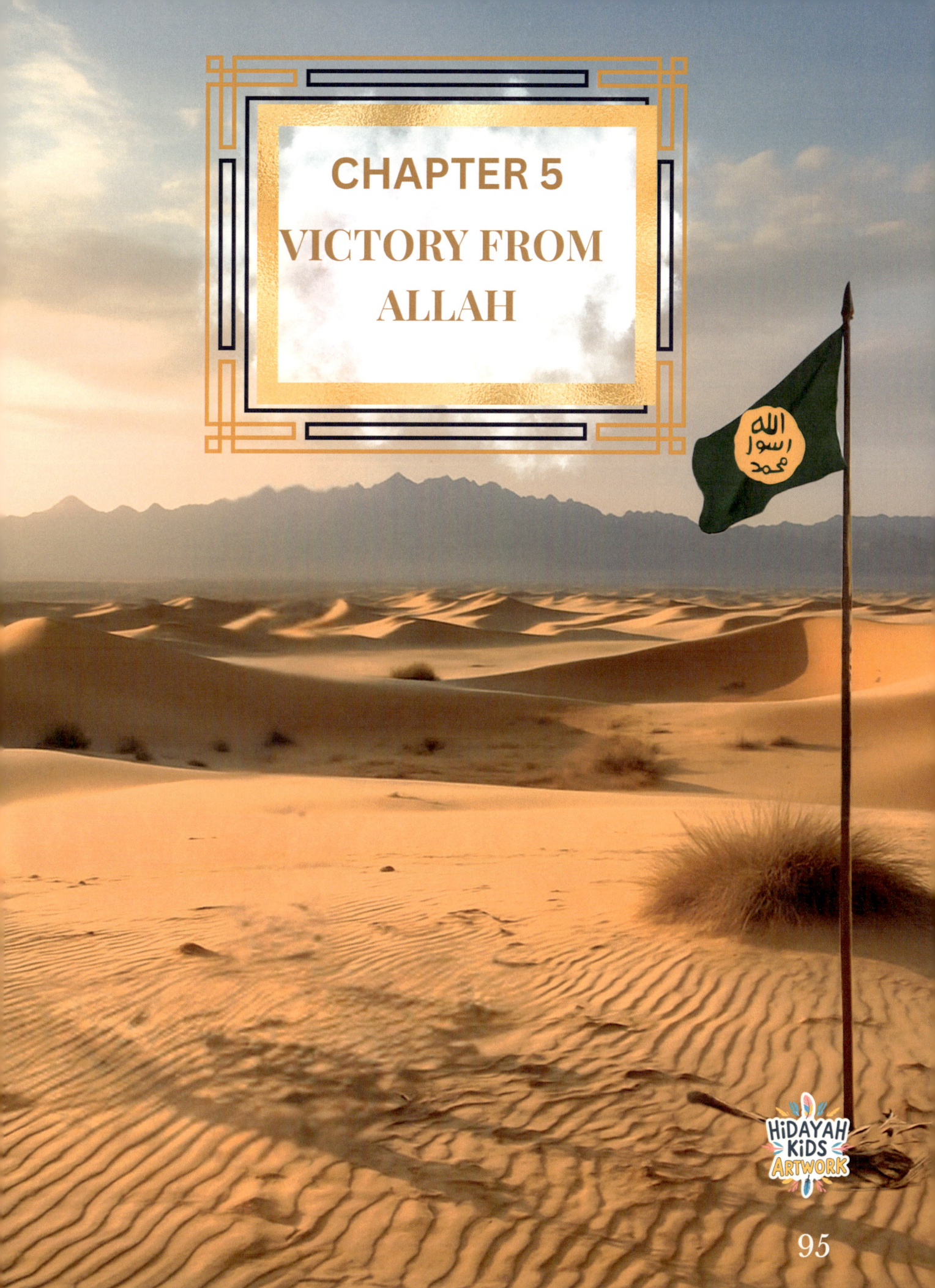
CHAPTER 5
VICTORY FROM ALLAH

The room was very quite today.

The scroll of Sa'd (R.A.) and Umair (R.A.) lay rolled beside them, as if even it was resting after such a heavy story from yesterday. Outside, the night deepened and the stars twinkled brighter.

Hidayah leaned forward, her voice just above a whisper:

"Some stories... stay in your heart for a long time."

She gently reached for the final scroll, her fingers slow and careful — as if she already knew this one was different.

"This is the last scroll," she said softly. "The story of how Allah's promise came true.

The Muslims won — not with swords or numbers.. but with du'ā and with hearts full of faith.

Ready?"

And just like that... the last chapter began.

"Victory from Allah."

 Victory from Allah

The battlefield was quiet now.
No more swords clashing.
No more cries of charge.
Only the soft wind and footsteps in the sand.
The Muslims — dusty, tired, and tearful — stood in silence.
But their hearts... were full.
It was time to see what Allah had written.
They had won.
It was hard to believe.
The enemy army had outnumbered them three to one.
They had more weapons, horses, and armour.
The Muslims had only 313 companions — most with no armour, some without swords.
But they had something else - the promise of Allah.
And Allah did not let them down.
Allah sent angels — unseen, powerful helpers from the heavens — just as He had promised.

Some companions said they heard voices from the sky.

> "On the Day of Badr, I saw an enemy struck down though no man was near him."
> — Tafsir al-Tabari, Surah Al-Anfal (8:12)

As the battle ended, Prophet Muhammad ﷺ stood quietly.

He looked at the battlefield... and looked to the sky.

Then he softly recited the verse revealed after their victory:

> "Allah had certainly made you victorious at Badr while you were few in number. So be mindful of Allah, that you may be grateful."
> — Surah Aali 'Imran (3:123)

His voice was calm. His eyes filled with tears — not of pride, but of shukr.

The companions gathered the fallen — those who had given their lives for the truth.

The First Martyrs

Not everyone who came to Badr returned home. Fourteen brave companions gave their lives for Islam. They were the first martyrs of the first great battle in Islam's history. Each one of them stood with courage, fighting not for fame or land, but for the truth and the love of Allah.

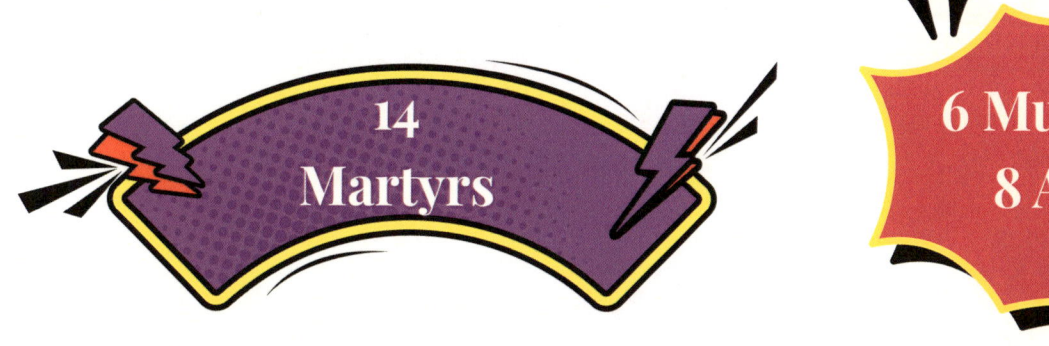

Six were from the Muhajirin (those who came from Makkah) were:

1. Ubaydah ibn al-Ḥarith (R.A.) – One of the first to be injured in battle

2. Aqil ibn al-Bukayr (R.A.),

3. Safwan ibn Bayḍa' (R.A.),

4. Dhū al-Shimālayn ʿAmr ibn ʿAbd ʿAmr

5. Umayr ibn Abi Waqqaṣ (R.A.) - Very young and brave companion; brother of Saʿd ibn Abī Waqqāṣ

6. Mihja ibn Ṣaliḥ (R.A.) – Known as the first martyr at Badr.

And eight from the Anṣar (the helpers of Madinah) were:

1. Ḥarithah ibn Suraqah (R.A.) - His mother asked the Prophet ﷺ about him, and she was told he reached Jannah
2. Sa'd ibn Khaythamah (R.A.)
3. Mu'awwidh ibn al-Ḥarith (R.A.) - One of the boys who attacked Abu Jahl
4. Awf ibn al-Ḥarith (R.A.) - His brother also fought bravely,
5. Yazid ibn al-Ḥarith (R.A.),
6. Mubashshir ibn Abd al-Mundhir (R.A.),
7. Rafi' ibn al-Mualla (R.A.), and
8. Umayr ibn al-Ḥammam (R.A.) - Famous for throwing away his dates and rushing into battle.

They are honoured as true heroes of Islam — and the Prophet Muhammad ﷺ said he would personally testify for them on the Day of Judgment.

— Musnad Aḥmad

Note: The names of the martyrs of Badr are documented in early sources such as Ṭabaqat Ibn Sad and al-Iṣabah by Ibn Ḥajar.

Then came the prisoners.

After the battle, the Muslims captured 70 prisoners of war — including leaders of disbelievers in Mecca. But instead of hurting them, the Prophet Muhammad ﷺ instructed the Muslims:

> "Treat the Prisoners well."
>
> — Bukhari (Al-Adab Al-Mufrad)

And many companions did just that.

Even in victory, the Muslims showed mercy.

Some companions, like Sayyiduna Abu Ayyub Al-Ansari (R.A.), gave the prisoners bread, while keeping dates for themselves (even when they themselves had little).

And the Qur'an praised this mercy:

"And they give food, out of love for Him (Allah), to the needy, the orphan, and the captive (prisoners of war)..."

— Tafsir al-Ṭabari, 76:8

The Muslims had won.
But they showed kindness, not cruelty.
Mercy, not revenge.
Because that's what true victory looks like.

When the army returned to Madinah, there was no loud celebration.
No banners. No parades.
They walked in with bowed heads and grateful hearts — because they knew it wasn't their strength that brought victory...

"Help and victory come only from Allah — the All-Mighty, the All-Wise."

Surah Al-Anfal (8:10)

What Made Them Real Superheroes?

The companions of Badr didn't have superpowers.
They had Iman.
And that was enough to change the world.

They didn't fly.
They didn't shoot webs or lift mountains.
They didn't wear glowing armor or magical rings.
But they had something stronger than all that.

They had:
- 🛡️ Truthfulness that never wavered.
- ⏳ Patience even when things were scary.
- 🤲 Loyalty to Prophet Muhammad ﷺ, no matter the cost.
- 🌙 Trust in Allah — in every moment, every step.
- ❤️ Kindness, even to people who once hurt them.

Because they knew that bravery isn't in capes or masks.
It's in character.
It's in choosing what's right — even when it's hard.

The lamp in the library flickered softly now, casting long, golden shadows across the scrolls and shelves. The last story had been read. The final words had settled like feathers on the air.

The friends sat close together on the cushions, no longer leaning forward with wide eyes… but leaning back, thinking of the Prophet ﷺ and his great companions.

A feeling of stillness wrapped around them — the kind that only comes after something important has been shared.

Hidayah's eyes moved slowly from the stars to her sisters and Shuja. She smiled.

Not the kind of smile that comes from a joke or a game. But the kind that comes when you know something has changed inside you — and you're not quite the same anymore.

The stories of Badr were over.

But their light… would stay.

Shujāʿ (blinking sleepily but sitting up):
"So... what happened after Badr? Did the Quraysh of Makkah give up?"

Hidayah (gently, holding the scroll close):
"Not quite. They became more angry. They wanted revenge and they started preparing for another battle — one even harder than Badr."

Emaan (curious):
"Another battle? So soon?"

Hidayah (nodding):
"Yes. It was called the Battle of Uhud which happened just one year after Badr. And do you know what happened? The battle was so fierce that Prophet Muhammad ﷺ himself got severely injured and a rumour spread across the battlefield... that the Prophet ﷺ had been killed."

Zarsha (stomping her little feet):
"Nooo! That's not true! He's the best-best!"
(She meant: the best of all humans — Prophet Muhammad ﷺ.)

Emaan (leaning forward, eyes full of wonder):
"What happened next? I can't wait!"

Hidayah:
"Well...that's for our next book... Super Muslim Heroes of Uhud — we'll meet more brave companions, witness their struggles, and see what happened after Badr."

Shujāʿ (with a grin):
"Just tell me there's a flying camel in the story."
They all shared gentle smiles, yet in their hearts, they reflected on the Prophet ﷺ and his unwavering struggle for the truth.

Glossary

Word	Meaning
Captive	A prisoner taken during battle
Sabr	Patience — staying calm and trusting Allah, even during tough times
Shukr (Gratitude)	Thanking Allah with your heart, words, and actions
Taqwa	Being aware of Allah in all your actions and staying on the right path
Mala'ika (Angels)	Beings made from light, who obey Allah completely and helped at Badr

Where did all these stories come from?

Everything you read in this book come from authentic Islamic books written by respected scholars, hundreds of years ago. These books tell us what truly happened in the time of the Prophet Muhammad ﷺ, and who stood with him in the most important battle in Islam: The Battle of Badr.

Here are the main books we used:
Historical & Biographical Books

📗 Sirah of Ibn Hisham

A famous book about the life of Prophet Muhammad ﷺ, including the Hijrah, the battles, and the bravery of his companions.

📙 Maghazi of al-Waqidi

One of the earliest books that tells the full stories of the battles the Prophet ﷺ took part in — like Badr and Uhud.

📘 **Tabaqat of Ibn Sa'd**

A collection of stories about the Prophet ﷺ and the people who followed him, especially focused on what they did and how they lived.

📙 **Al-Bidayah wa al-Nihayah by Ibn Kathir**

A book of Islamic history from the beginning of creation to the stories of the Prophets and companions.

Hadith Books (Sayings of the Prophet ﷺ)

📗 Sahih al-Bukhari
📘 Sahih Muslim
📙 Sunan Abi Dawud
📘 Sunan al-Tirmidhi

These are part of the most authentic and well-known six books of hadith, called the "Sihah Sitta (The Six Sound Collections)."

These books collect the most trusted sayings and actions of Prophet Muhammad ﷺ. Scholars around the world use them to teach and explain Islam.

📘 Musnad Ahmad

A large hadith book that organizes sayings by which companion narrated them — so we learn what different Sahabah remembered about the Prophet ﷺ.

📗 Mustadrak al-Ḥakim

This book includes authentic hadith that were not found in the earlier famous books. The author carefully checked them for truth and accuracy.

Tafsir Books (Quran's Explanation)

📙 Tafsir Ibn Kathir

One of the most trusted tafsir books — helps us understand the meaning of Qur'an verses through authentic hadith.

📖 Tafsir al-Tabari

One of the earliest and most comprehensive tafsir books — it explains Qur'an verses using reports from the Prophet ﷺ, the Companions, and early scholars.

A LETTER TO YOU YOUNG MUSLIM SUPERHERO

Dear reader,

You've just walked through the sands of Badr. You've seen a small army with big hearts. You've stood beside young superheroes who were fearless, But do you know something special?

This story isn't just about them. It's about you too.

You might never be on a battlefield…But every single day, you face your own little battles.

And every time you choose what's right — even when it's hard…

Every time you stay kind… or speak the truth…

Or stand up for someone who's hurting…

That's bravery.

That's character.

That's being a hero in Allah's eyes.

Every time you choose honesty, kindness, patience, or prayer…

Remember that you are walking the path of Badr. You belong to an ummah of the brave. And your heart is stronger than you know.

With Love,

Hidayah Asfand

The story teller behind "Super Muslim Heroes Series".

What's Next?

Super Muslim Heroes Series - Book 2

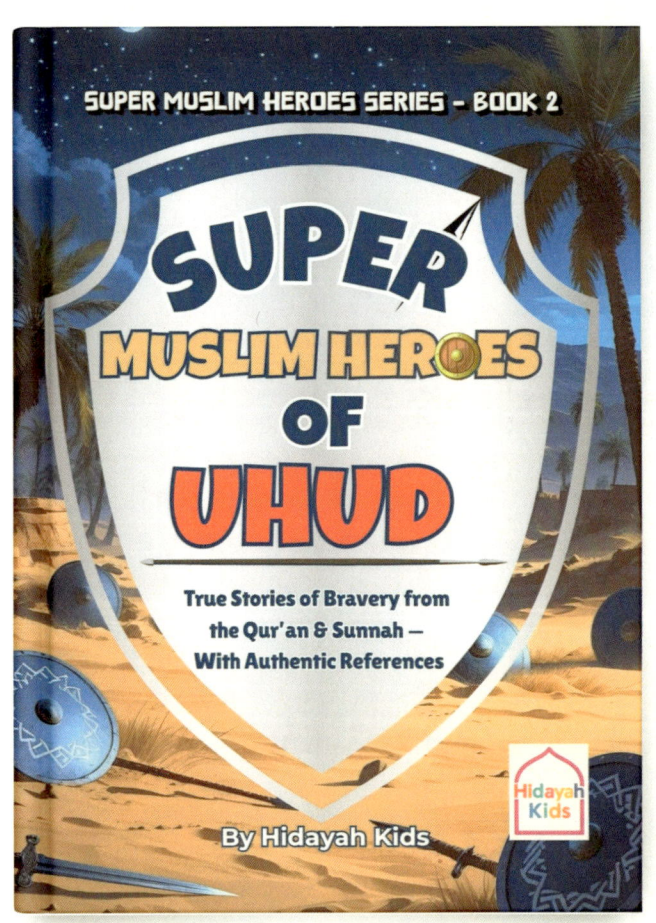

Muslim Superhero Missions

Your Muslim Superhero Missions

- 💬 Speak the truth, even when no one else does. ☑

- 🤝 Help a friend who's left out or alone. ☑

- 🕋 Pray on time — even when you feel shy or lazy. ☑

- 🩷 Tell your siblings, "Don't worry, Let's make du'a". ☑

- 🌙 Whisper "Allah u Akbar" when you feel scared. ☑

- 📖 Open the Qur'an when your heart feels heavy. ☑

- 🕌 Wake up for Fajr, even when it's freezing. ☑

Your Muslim Superhero Missions

⭐ 8 — 🙇 Say "I'm sorry" — even when it's tough. ☐

⭐ 9 — 🍎 Share your snack with others. ☐

⭐ 10 — 🫶 Forgive — even when they didn't say sorry. ☐

⭐ 11 — 😔 Be patient when someone takes your turn. ☐

⭐ 12 — 🧕 Wear your hijab proudly, even when no one else is. ☐

⭐ 13 — Say "No" when others are doing something wrong. ☐

⭐ 14 — 📿 Remember Allah — even when you're alone. ☐

Other Books by Hidayah Kids

Sunnah Series Book 1

Noora the Sleepy Star

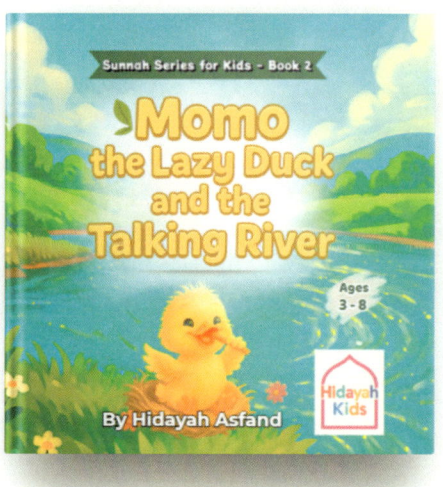

Sunnah Series Book 2

Momo the Lazy Duck and the Talking River

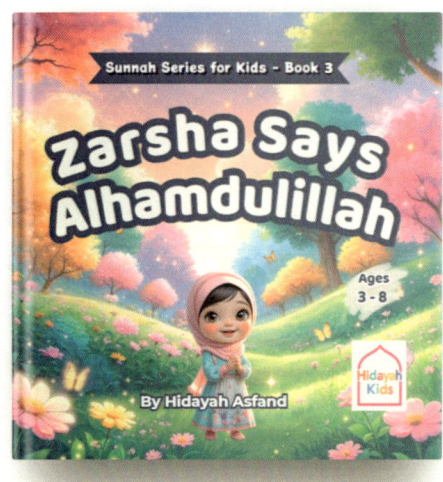

Sunnah Series Book 3

Zarsha Says Alhamdolilah

BADR SUPERHERO CERTIFICATE

This certificate is proudly presented to

_____

for completing the book and all the Muslim Superhero missions (Badr) and proving a heart full of:

- Faith
- Courage
- Kindness, and
- Love for Allah and His Prophet ﷺ

You are now an "Honorary Badr Muslim Superhero".
May your deeds shine like stars in the sky,
and may Allah ﷻ make you brave like Umair (R.A), strong like Sa'd (R.A), and wise like Barrah (R.A).

Signed with love by:
Hidayah & Shujāʿ – the baby camel

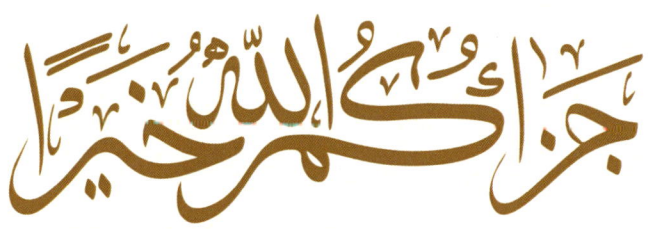

www.ingramcontent.com/pod-product-compliance
Lightning Source LLC
Chambersburg PA
CBRC091206010526
44107CB00021B/1256